The Committee To Save The World

SELECTED LITERARY NONFICTION

by Robert Day

Introdcution by Wes Jackson, President, The Land Institute
Foreword by Bob Thompson, *Washington Post*

Paintings by Kathryn Jankus Day

Books by Robert Day:

The Last Cattle Drive (a novel)
Speaking French in Kansas (short fiction)
We Should Have Come by Water (poetry)

Printed in the United States.

Published in 2009 by Western Books,
PO Box 1, Woodston, KS 67675, 888-321-7341.

Library of Congress Control Number 2009938244
ISBN 978-0-938463-09-2
Cover illustration by Kathryn Jankus Day. Title of Piece, media used, size.
Kathryn Jankus Day is represented by Strecker-Nelson Gallery
in Manhattan, Kansas.
Book design by Diane Landskroener.

Printed by Mennonite Press, North Newton, Kansas.

The Committee To Save The World

*This Book is for Wes and Joan Jackson,
and Leo and Bonita Oliva.*

And for Kathryn Jankus Day.

Acknowledgements

"Not in Kansas Anymore," "High Plains Drifters," "Fox Hunting," and "The Radio Game" were originally published by the *Washington Post Sunday Magazine;* "Carrie Nation" was first published by *Smithsonian Magazine;* "The Family Dog" by *Modern Maturity,* "*The Last Cattle Drive* Stampede" by *KS Magazine;* "Nabokov" by the *Kansas City Star;* "Wind, Water, Fact and Fiction" by *World Literature Today,* and "The Committee to Save the World" by *New Letters.*

"The Route of *The Last Cattle Drive*" was commissioned by The University Press of Kansas for the 30th Anniversary Edition of *The Last Cattle Drive* (University Press of Kansas, 2007) and is printed therein as "Some Notes on the Writing of *The Last Cattle Drive*: Or My Life as Fiction."

"I Look Out for Ed Wolf" and "Parts of Their Nights: An Elegy for Our Professors" were *festschrifts*, republished in *Cottonwood Review* and *Parts of Their Nights.*

"The Scholar and Artist Homestead Act for 21st-Century America," "Ode to Red," "Talk to Strangers and Stop on By," "The Last Tank of Gasoline in America," "'It Was Snowing,'" and "I Get a Horse" were all commissioned for and distributed by The Prairie Writers Circle of The Land Institute, Salina, Kansas.

The author's literary representative is Russell and Volkening, Inc., New York City.

Contents

Introduction

Bob Day and I both grew up in Kansas at a time of several weekly 30-minute radio programs. My favorite hero was Straight Arrow. The program opened with: "A gleaming arrow set against a rawhide string. A strong bow bent almost to the breaking point and then" followed by a sound that told us rapt listeners that the arrow had been released. We could hear the arrow sailing through the air and then the thump indicating it had hit its intended target. Following the thump the narrator would announce the program with a simple "Straight Arrow." I'm sure that the arrow served as a metaphor for correct behavior in a subliminal sort of way.

Straight Arrow, Dick Tracy, The Fat Man, The Shadow, The Lone Ranger, Hopalong Cassidy—these programs were about more than "crime does not pay." Generally featured was a moral order.

Straight Arrow was not like the masked Lone Ranger. Straight Arrow had a regular job. I know this because every week the narrator would remind us that, "To friends and neighbors alike, Steve Adams was the young owner of the Broken Bow cattle spread. But when danger threatened innocent people (music: duh, duh, duh-da) and when evildoers plotted against justice (music again: duh, duh, duh-da), then Steve Adams, rancher, disappeared and in his place came a mysterious, stalwart Indian whose horse was stabled in a "vast subordinate cave." At least that's the way I remembered it. I do wonder how a cave could be anything but subordinate. The narrator continued, "The walls of the cave glitter with crystals of gold." "The light spreads a shimmering gleam everywhere, and standing in the golden light is the great golden palomino, Fury." Fury would whinny at this point, causing Straight Arrow to say, "Steady there, Big Horse." Shortly we heard, "Riding out of the darkness to take up the cause of law and order throughout the West comes the legendary figure of Straight Arrow." No matter that the horse in a cave stable had been standing in the golden light due to the walls of the cave being covered with crystals of gold—at those memorable lines goosebumps appeared on my arms.

Straight Arrow was my favorite. I have never asked Bob Day what his was, but both of us grew up with such radio programs. All had moral lessons. To assess the quality of this oral literary effort goes beyond my pay scale. They took place during WWII and a little after, until television killed them (The Lone Ranger was never as good on the screen as on the radio).

I tell you of this time in America to prepare you for the little pieces of this volume which illustrate that this distant past helped shape Bob Day's neural network mostly in the frontal lobe, I suspect. He admits that early development influenced his literary sense. Right off he tells us that as a young reader in Kansas, having read *The Adventures of Don Quixote de la Mancha,* he believed that "Don Quixote had a better view of the world than Sancho Panza." Of course he believed that. The heroes of that time—on a horse if they were knights—made truth and justice appealing. No matter that Cervantes is writing a spoof on the dying age of chivalry. Bob Day is still susceptible.

He is proud of his cowboyhood, believes in truth and justice. If Bob Day did not have a horse named Rocinante (the name of

Don Quixote's horse, in case you, dear reader, have forgotten) he should have. What we have in this volume is Bob Day riding Rocinante II, approaching each of us as a modern Knight Errant while flattering us with his erudition, all the while remembering Cervantes' line, "Let them eat the lie and swallow it with their bread."

Bob Day lives part of his life in southwestern France and part of it not far from the Kansas-Colorado line in a tiny town he calls Bly. Now there is a combination. This Bly-spirit of Day lives in a town several months of the year not all that far from the land of Don Quixote. Forget the 400 years which have passed since Rocinante the First carried Don Quixote and set the standard for a former day which influenced our Bob Day in our day.

In your hands you have the writings of a man with a comparable sense of oughtness to Don Quixote's. As you read, be mindful of those radio programs that featured knights on horseback and the Knight errant. I would not have been surprised to have read in this piece Knight errant Day saying something similar to Don Quixote's, "All of which is now so clear in my mind that it bids me, persuades me, and even compels me, to demonstrate to you the purpose for which Heaven has sent me into the world and made me profess therein the order of chivalry which I follow, and the vow I made to succor the needy and those who are oppressed by the strong."

Knight Day in our time knows there is a gathering storm and, like his spiritual ancestor, "for everything which he saw he adapted with great facility to his wild, chivalrous and errant fancies."

There is one contradiction in these otherwise apt comparisons. Don Quixote said, "Away with those who say that Letters have the advantage over Arms!" Bob Day is a man of letters. But he is also a reincarnation of Don Quixote, Straight Arrow, Hopalong Cassidy, The Lone Ranger and Tom Mix. And should we ask him to explain, I would not be surprised to hear him quote his oldest guru: "The reason for the unreason with which you treat my reason, so weakens my reason that with reason I complain."

Now it's time for you to tune in where out of the present come the thundering hoof beats of the horses ridden by members of the Committee to Save the World.

—Wes Jackson

Foreword

When the late Richard Harwood first suggested that his friend Robert Day should write for the *Washington Post Magazine,* my heart sank. Which just goes to show how wrong an editor's instincts can be.

This was in the spring of 1989. I was a relative newcomer to the *Post* who had recently been asked to take over the magazine. Dick Harwood was a *Post* veteran, far senior to me, whose status as an ex-Marine always seemed to come up when his name was mentioned.

Oh great, I thought. I'm being bigfooted. As Dick handed me a manila envelope filled with clips, I was preemptively mulling how to explain that his Kansas-bred pal—what was that book he'd written? "The Last Cattle Drive?"—just wasn't good enough.

Then I read the clips. Harwood, it turned out, had more complex taste than that leatherneck stereotype implied.

A few months later, Bob filed his first piece for the magazine. I gave it to my smart art director to read. He liked it, but he had a question.

"Are we really going to publish this?" he asked.

I didn't blame him. "Not in Kansas Anymore," as you can see for yourself, was utterly different from the kind of stories that normally appeared in Sunday magazines. These tended not to begin with angry, bearded men reading newspapers aloud to the FBI building, and not to include advice like: "Don't let the bone in your head get bent. Bent head bones can lead to rounded edges, polished boots, fashionable women and trucks with stereos in them. It is thought you can disappear into such a world and never be seen again as yourself."

In the six years that followed, Bob would write more than a dozen articles for the *Post Magazine*. It is possible, in retrospect, to place them in distinct categories.

There were pieces in which Bob appeared as a stranger in strange lands. In one, he evoked the unique culture of the Eastern Shore of Maryland, a place where he knew—despite having spent two decades teaching there—that he would never, ever, be accepted as "local." That didn't stop him from sketching portraits of Shore neighbors whose roots went back to 1705, or from noticing "small lovelinesses in the Eastern Shore language" such as what you say when a horse is seriously ill (you say he has "lost the use of his self"). Later, Bob explored the genteelly bizarre world of Virginia fox hunting from the perspective of a "displaced stockman from the Western High Plains of America" with a penchant for socially inappropriate jokes.

"We may be lepers after this one," his wife, Kathy, confided.

There were pieces in which Bob channeled George Plimpton, notably the one in which the *Washington Post* paid him to take flying lessons and he lived to tell the tale. Nice work if you can get it—and if you have the kind of flight instructor who calmly says "I have the plane" and takes the controls when you're about to botch a landing.

There were a couple of enlightening pieces on teaching, an art form Bob takes almost as seriously as writing, and not just because it pays more of his bills. With luck, "Tales Out of School" will be included in some future Robert Day collection.

"Mainly they think about sex" is how it began.

Finally, there were articles built around childhood and memory, including an especially lovely piece that turned out to be the last thing Bob wrote before I stopped editing the magazine in 1995. "The Radio Game" was about baseball, among other things, and a long-ago Kansas summer when, with adulthood looming, the author's father revealed to him the facts of life.

Young Bob learned about the origin of puppies, a topic the elder Day approached "in a roundabout way." More important, he learned that the radio broadcasts of Kansas City Blues base-ball games were faked, Ronald Reagan style, by announcers who took a bare-bones enumeration of hits, walks and strikeouts off a studio ticker tape and turned it into a dramatic narrative "com-plete with prerecorded crowd noise and bat whacks."

What a lesson for a future fiction writer—and what a caution-ary tale for an editor trying to publish that writer's work in a non-fiction magazine. But by the time he wrote "The Radio Game," Bob knew exactly how to finesse the problematic line between a newspaper's idea of facts and a storyteller's notion of truth: "Full disclosure here," he wrote. "Everything I have written thus far is true the way radio baseball is true." And so it was.

Since acquiring the secret of the radio game, Bob has spent a lifetime enhancing the ticker tape of experience with the bat whacks of imagination. As any good writer can tell you, it's hard work and it usually doesn't pay.

But if you do it right, as this collection shows, it can keep the bone in your head from getting bent.

—Bob Thompson

"Hemingway"

Author's Note:
The Magazine Pieces

For a number of years in the 1990s I wrote for a variety of magazines—*Modern Maturity, Smithsonian, Forbes, FYI, KS Magazine, Regardies*—but mainly for *The Washington Post Magazine* where the editor Bob Thompson noted I was a "chronic contributor." He smiled when he said it, but he laughed out loud when I proposed doing a story about me trying to join the Chevy Chase Club.

Not in Kansas Anymore

The man on Pennsylvania Avenue is reading *The Washington Post* to the FBI building: It doesn't seem to be listening. The man in question is bearded and angry, although the anger has taken on that cynical clip you no doubt acquire if you read *The Washington Post* to the FBI building over a very long time and it begins to dawn on you it is a building that doesn't listen.

"As the name indicates," goes the angry bearded man to the FBI building, thumping *The Post* with his index finger and reading as though reciting verse, "photo radar/ will be a device/ to take pictures/ of the license plates/ and the drivers of vehicles/ exceeding posted speed limits/ by more than a significant set amount."

Behind him, a mammoth crane is backing up, a *now-hear-this-or-die* beeper blaring away; its huge bucket swings in the air. Two women scurry down the sidewalk, one talking of Jesse Helms, polyester suits and photographs of naked black men she has just seen in a nearby museum. Across the street, a platinum limousine, roughly the size of Southern California and with a device that resembles a miniature stealth bomber mounted on its roof, is negotiating the most sweeping U-turn in the history of western civilization. Traffic backs up to all our embassies in all the corners of the earth.

"Photo radar," the man continues, "would reduce the instances/ in which officers must approach cars." Here he pauses and looks over the edge of *The Post* with the meaningful gaze of a Berkeley philosophy major circa 1968. Still no response from the FBI building. The platinum limousine has completed its half-the-globe semicircle and double-parked beside the crane, which, although standing still, continues to bleat away, as if going backward is the *idée fixe* of its existence. Overhead, three low-flying helicopters rattle toward the Potomac in a self-important formation. No one gets in or out of the platinum limousine; it idles like a casket. Down the sidewalk, two men, both carrying what appear to be water buffalo brief cases from State Department assignments in Goa, walk by in conversation about the "arrogant stiffness" of a local Italian wine store: "One should never recommend an '80 Biondi-Santi Brunello even if one's father does know the owner." But of course. Tell it to the black windows of the platinum limousine, tell it to the philosophy major reading *The Washington Post* to the FBI building. Tell it to Jesse Helms. Dan Quayle. Tell it to me. It will remind me I'm not in Kansas anymore.

Kansas? Do I make a cheap joke at the expense of Toto, Bob Dole, Marshal Dillon and all the other *faux naif* knockabouts who claim to inhabit that fictional black-and-white square of wheat and populism somewhere west of Falls Church? No joke at all. Kansas is real, sort of. In fact I've just come back from a year out there only to descend into the equally "sort of real" world of Washington, D.C. and its environs.

It's a potent drink, these mixed realities: dry martinis at Nathan's, whiskey and tomato beer at the Palomino Tavern in Hays, Kansas. But drink up: This story is about you—especially if you are no more from Pennsylvania Avenue and the pastures that surround it than am I. Together we will find a small truth in the text here abounds, to wit: You *can* go home again; it's leaving more than once that gets tricky.

"Is that true, Bobby?"

"It is," I say. I am talking to my neighbor Banger. Banger lives in the back of a '60s Pontiac station wagon that he has buried nose first in the side of a low hill on his hardscrabble ranch. The buffalo grass has restitched itself over the trench Banger had to dig; if there is rain in the spring, small prairie flowers bloom on the ground above the hood. You don't know Banger and his car are there unless you come at them from the east and can see the back end open in the hill, the tail gate down.

We are in western Kansas. It is late summer. Already it has been 106° in the sun. We don't measure heat in the shade in western Kansas because we don't have much shade, which is why Banger has buried his station wagon: The earth is Shade City. Besides, a big suburban station wagon has ranch house space: Banger sleeps in the middle seat, reads in the front, and watches the world go by out of the back-facing rear seat. A three room "deal" is what he calls it.

In winter, Banger moves himself to his one-man A-frame, complete with a wood burner, two windows and not much more. It's down in a draw so the November through April wind doesn't eat him alive. In some final version of Banger's dream estate, he wants to have his entire deal underground: The earth, he says, is a "thermal battery. Cool in summer. Warm in winter." In his mind he sees one day a stovepipe sticking up through the sod, puffing cottonwood smoke out into the blue white of Januarys. But the best things in life take time. That's okay by Banger. Time's free.

"So," Banger says just to get it straight, "when they tear down a building in Our Nation's Capital, they leave up the wall that's on the street." Banger is asking about "facadism" —that distinctly urban practice, begun a few years back, whereby Washington and other cities started saving the fronts of their historic buildings while tearing down everything else.

"That's right," I say. In Kansas, Washington, D.C., is always called

"Our Nation's Capital," a phrase we learned in high school civics classes and continue to use in the hope that language alone will keep the Circle City of Government true.

I am being questioned about life in Washington because the men out here—Banger among them—know I've spent 20 years in and around Our Nation's Capital, and they are curious, in their direct way, about what it is like. It is also true I have just spent the previous year among them, living with my wife in a small cabin we keep on the high plains as an amulet against the fury of civilization. Why Banger is asking about facadism, how he has come to know about it at all, or why it interests him, he does not say. The month before—when Banger and I helped a friend move cattle—he wanted to know about the "hill" of Capitol Hill: its size, sidewalks, trees and what you could see from there once you climbed to the top. Now, Banger considers his new line of questioning by looking at his beer and then, for a moment, out at the yellow buffalo grass that is his 2,000-acre lawn.

"And the reason they leave the front that's on the street side when they tear down the building," asks Banger in a flat voice that keeps irony at bay, "is because they made themselves a law that tells them to do that."

"That's right," I say. "It's to keep the past alive. History."

We are silent for a moment while Banger thinks about this. Heat on the prairie has no noise. The nearest road is miles away. The station wagon has a lean-to canvas porch out the back of it. Banger stirs slightly on the tailgate. I am sitting in a stock saddle draped on a square bale. Just beyond us is a foot-long section of pipeline iron that has been converted into a cooking grill. Off in the shelter belt—a circle of trees that protects home places against the wind—you can see a shovel with a roll of toilet paper slid down over its broken handle. If you walked up the hill to the west above Banger's deal, you might catch the distant ka-thud of some doctor-lawyer oil well, but probably not. Overhead, contrails etch the sky for a while, then fray like old rope. Nothing that just passes through this country is remembered. Coming and going in the Russian olives and dusty cedars of the shelter belt are turtledoves. If you were down there, you could hear them cooing.

"Now," says Banger, "suppose you wanted to have a vacant lot behind the building you tear down in Our Nation's Capital where you could keep a horse on a cinder block."

"Yes," I say.

"Would you still have to leave the front of your building standing?"

"You would," I say.

"History," he says.

"Yes," I say.

"And the windows," he says. "Would they still be in the building that's history?"

"They would," I say. "In the front."

"So if you don't want anyone to look at your horse on the cinder block in your back yard, you can pull the shades in the windows?"

"You can," I say.

"And that wouldn't be against the law about history and the front of the building?" he says.

"No," I say. "Only you wouldn't have any way to pull the shades on the top floors."

"No stairs," says Banger.

"They'd be gone," I say.

"I see," Banger says. He grins.

The trick out here is not to let on exactly what's so funny.

"*Pull the shades and light the light, I'll be home late tonight.*" He doesn't sing it, he just says it.

Banger and I have known each other for a very long time. He is worried that living on the East Coast might have re-arranged the bone in my head. That's what we say out on the High Plains when someone has lost sight of the singular madness that is necessary to get from the January blizzards to the May tornadoes, and from there to the August branding irons—all on beans and rice, a little whiskey, and no doubt some crooked cigarettes: *Don't let the bone in your head get bent.* Bent head bones can lead to rounded edges, polished boots, fashionable women and trucks with stereos in them. It is thought you can disappear into such a world and never be seen again as yourself.

Banger eases off the tailgate and climbs forward into the bowels of his station wagon. He settles in behind the steering wheel and looks at the dirt packed up against the windshield. The earth's weight has cracked the glass like a star, but it does not sag. Banger's dash is a shelf for paperbacks. He punches in a cigarette lighter that still works; he loves the modernity of it. From over the visor he takes his rolling papers and, looking into the mirror, says:

"You going back?"

"I am," I say. "I've come to tell you so."

"I know you have," he says.

"Going to leave the end of the week," I say.   .

"Will you give me a hand before you go?" he says.

"Bull calves?" I say.

"The ones we didn't cut last fall," he says. He has rolled his smoke and burns the end of it with the car lighter. Bits of paper curl in flame and fall away as ash. I can see him in the mirror, grinning through the smoke.

"I'll give you the calf-fries to take along when you go," he says. "Prairie oysters once a week keep the bone in your head from getting bent. It's medically proven."

"I believe it is," I say.

It has been a long, deadly drive across the country from Kansas to D.C. Interstates are the straight white teeth of the pretty people who have the conversation of cheerleaders or television actors.

Coming down 270 off the Pennsylvania Turnpike, my wife and I are trying to recall how the Beltway works:

"Some of the government gets out at 4," she says, "Or is it 3?" Neither of us remembers, and, although it is a matter of timing to avoid "the crunch," the question is moot because neither of us has a watch and our truck's clock is stuck at 8:32, which is when we dropped the front end over a washout in Banger's pasture the morning before we left. We are south of Frederick and coming in; and we are getting lost in some way we don't fully understand.

Our sense is that the plethora of German cars streaming around us have corporate jet cockpits complete with various liquid crystal rectangles that flash Time of Arrival, Miles Per Gallon, Average Trip Speed, as well as other useful and urgent data. We have heard there are television maps on board these days. We imagine for a moment that by the lightest touch on the tiniest slate gray button in our truck we can project ourselves onto a deep green cathode ray tube carved with red and yellow corridors. A chart of our whereabouts. We see ourselves, a throbbing white dot, coming back from someplace not on the map.

In the left lane, a Mercedes Man who has ebbed and flowed beside us for three or four miles is in earnest conversation on a cell phone. He is shaking his head "no" and pounding the steering wheel with his free hand: A promotion has been denied; a deal sprung loose; a senator backed into a corner. Command is hell, lonely. But that's what you get two hundred-plus K for. Ahead, he spots an opening and surges beyond us onto bright white lanes just opened. Nothing we see looks all that familiar.

"I hear," says Banger as he sits in his front seat smoking, but looking straight ahead now and not in the mirror, "that Bob Dole has his own parking place."

"He does," I say.

"And more than one office."

"Probably," I say.

"Which means more than one parking place."

"Probably," I say. We stop to think. Then:

"Has anyone told Bob Dole," says Banger, "about the woman in Russell who talks to St. Peter in her basement?" Russell, Kan., is Bob Dole's hometown.

"I don't think so," I say."

"St. Peter tells her Bob Dole's going to be the next and last president of the United States. Maybe he should know."

"I think you're right," I say.

"Sometimes," Banger says, "I sit up here and imagine I'm driving through the earth of America." He puts both hands on the wheel.

"Where do you go?" I say.

"I have some Blood Indians I know near Browning, Montana," he says.

"Why don't you drive back to see me?"

"To Our Nation's Capital?" He looks up into the mirror.

"Yes," I say.

"Where would I park?" he says.

Ten miles out from the beltway and descending into a thick fog of brown construction dust and grimy traffic, we begin to spin the radio dial: Bach fugues; Mayor Barry and cocaine; Handel's Water Music; someone has shot his wife and children to death, then shot himself but lives, comatose; a new book on lobbyists in Washington has been published; Saint Saëns through Stravinsky; a full report on world events at 6. And everywhere on every airwave, some traffic artery that we thought was blocked the year we left is blocked again—or still. It is, we learn, Three-Oh-Seven in the afternoon. And counting.

Coming into it finally, we wonder if we'll remember which ramps and loops and lanes navigate us east around the Beltway toward College Park, instead of south toward Cabin John: both places where we have never been—now that we think of it—and where we have no friends. Indeed, it occurs to us that most signs off the Beltway point toward strange lands, and although we know roughly where we are in our mind's eye, we know as well that the memory of our mind's eye is no match for the sprawling reality of the urban planner. New slabs of concrete create different horizons: In a circle of a city, who checks the sun to see which way you are going?

Ahead, in the traffic of one government or another, it turns out we make the correct banks and turns to find ourselves stalled in the direction we wanted to go. More dial spinning. More Bach. Some Mozart. A story about the buffalo commons: In the next decades the High Plains will become "depopulated." Buffalo is low-cholesterol meat. It grills nicely in Potomac over low coals. It eats its own grass and is natural to its area. No hormones. No steroids. Great herds will be visible out both sides of the aircraft on the morning flights to the West Coast. The larger towns of the plains will be fenced in. History circles back to life. We clutch and brake. Ahead are hills of cars. More Mozart. The familiar hostility of talk show radio.   .

"Is it true," says Banger, "what they say about the buffalo?"

We are standing by his working shed; the dust from the steers has settled. A bucket of prairie oysters is hanging from a harness hook where the barn cats can't get them. It is noon. Maybe.

"What about the buffalo?" I say.

"That the government's going to bring them back," he says.

"I don't know about that," I say. "What do you mean?"

"They think we're going belly up out here because everybody's leaving."

"Everybody *is* leaving," I say. "What's that got to do with the buffalo?"

"Just 'cause you're leaving," says Banger, "doesn't mean I'm leaving." He points at his chest "I'm here." Behind him some prairie chickens rise as a covey and flap and glide deep into the pastures. Sometimes you don't know what to say and it feels good.

"Do you know about the buffalo?" I say to the man reading *The Washington Post* to the FBI building. He will not catch my eye. "They're coming back to Kansas." There is a ricochet of light in the street: Someone has gotten in or out of the platinum limousine, but no one has seen it happen.

"Do you know how you drive to Montana in the earth of America?" I go on. Nothing. "Have you heard about St. Peter and Bob Dole?" Still nothing. Maybe he thinks he is on "The Oprah Winfrey Show" and, being male, it is best to keep quiet. "Pull the shades and light the light?" I say. The platinum limousine rocks slightly and moves off, commanding traffic. I realize I am worried about the bone in my head getting bent. I wonder if the man I'm talking to has taken the cure.

"Have you ever seen history in a horse tied to a cinder block behind a building that has only its front?" I say, this time more to the FBI building than anyone else. "The earth is a thermal battery," I go on. "Photo radar has not recorded Banger's deal. We all come from Kansas."

The man who reads *The Washington Post* to the FBI building hands me his paper and walks down the sidewalk. I'd take it with me back home, but on Pennsylvania Avenue in Our Nation's Capital, who can see a rainbow, much less find a Yellow Brick Road?

Fox Hunting

"What happens when you catch the fox?" I ask.

It is the evening's party after a long day's hunt on the final weekend (the last in March) of Virginia's fox-hunting season. The 18th-century farmhouse near Middleburg where I am a guest is laced with rich brandy and elegant men and women. I am sitting by the fire talking foxes and hounds and matters equestrian with my host, a man who is graciously guiding me through both the turf and language of what is simply called The Hunt. He seems slightly reserved about the matter, as if he feels he shouldn't be talking about the rituals of his endowed society. For my part, as a displaced stockman from the Western High Plains of America, I am all ears—dubious ears to be sure.

There is, I have learned—am learning as I listen to my host—more to The Hunt than foxes and horses and hounds. More even than the circle of sports (steeplechases, trail rides, dressage and the like) that have grown up around The Hunt. Taken together these events create a culture—not a populist culture, as it turns out, but then even the lordly get to play in the sunshine of a democracy.

"You don't catch the fox," says my host. It 'goes to ground'—usually in a woodchuck hole. When that happens both the hounds and the field come up. That's when you bring on Jack Russell."

"Who's Jack Russell?" I ask. I'm thinking he might have been the one who married Elizabeth Taylor.

"A tiny terrier," my host says, "that the riding groom carries in a shirt pouch."

"I see," I say. It seems slightly absurd that you would deliberately gallop a horse around with a dog in your pocket, but what do I know?

"The groom rides up to where the pack has gathered, gets off and puts Jack Russell by the hole with the fox in it"

"Why?" I ask. I am not playing dumb.

"Well," says my host, "a Jack Russell is a small feisty hound whose life's work is to dive down the front door of the woodchuck holes and pop foxes out back doors. Jack Russell is a specialist."

"Like a consultant," I say, "to the government."

"I wouldn't know," says my host. "I try not to attend Washington; I prefer horse country."

The "horse country" my host prefers lies to the west and south of Washington along routes 50 and 55 in Clarke and Fauquier counties. In the distance you can see the Blue Ridge, and there are horses and foxes and riders to the hounds in that country as well. But the best is said to be among these modest hills and finger woods.

It all seems richly English in flavor and color. You imagine the Cotswolds; Upper and Lower Slaughter. The fieldstone walls cut the land into something more like plots than pastures. In winter and early spring the most striking features are the huge, lovely, bare sycamore trees, their great trunks and limbs making a patchwork of light gray and snowy white, as if they had some appaloosa in them. The country roads are painterly: Constable or early Gainsborough. It is astonishing that anyone who has lived among such studied beauty ever left. Many have not.

"What happens after the fox goes out the back door?" I ask. I had seen nothing of Jack Russell or the fox going to ground earlier in the day when I had been driven around from farm to farm in hopes that I'd catch sight of The Hunt itself in progress. It is true that from time to time I'd spot what looked like a Founder's Day parade going through the fields and along the edges of the splendid woods and delicate creeks. It was as if some spur-and-saddle club of Hill City, Kansas had gotten lost on the way to the fairgrounds.

"When the fox runs," says my host, "the master of the hounds and his hunt staff start the chase. The field follows with the riding groom and Jack Russell taking up the rear."

For some reason the vision of the riding groom being left behind with tiny Jack Russell tucked into his shirt allows me to see the hunt in all its clamor and ruckus. I become the riding groom: Before me go black coats and red coats, hunting bowlers, gold-pinned stocks and Bedford cloth breeches—all on sleek horses 17 hands high, their riders calling out, "Tallyho, tallyho, tallyho." Jack Russell and I are not sure we should be members of a club that would have us as members, even if we are where we belong, at the back of the pack.

"What kind of dogs do you use in the pack?" I ask.

My host lights a thin black cigar, which I notice is not the Wolf Brothers stogie or the Mississippi Crooks favored in the ranch houses of Two Sleeps or Buffalo Gap or Spotted Horse—favored, I might point out, because they bring the rich flavor of the calving stalls to the dinner table and the talk.

"There are no 'dogs' in the pack," my host says, "only 'hounds.'" He looks at me to see if I understand the difference.

I make an effort. I think about the nature of dogs and hounds. In my mind's eye a number of dogs from my past crop up—good dogs all, none of them bad, none would bite a child, all would bite a wicked witch. As I think about it, my dogs have been dogs through and through, and none of them was ever a hound. When I think hounds, I see Lyndon Johnson.

"And they don't have tails," says my host as he exhales an obedient strip of smoke.

"What?" I say.

"Hounds don't have tails," he says.

I hope this is the opening gambit of a raw joke because I know quite a few good ones myself and I am looking for a chance to tell them but am not sure about my manners.

"What do hounds have?" I ask.

"They have sterns."

"Sterns?" I say.

"Sterns. Which they wave. A hound does not wag his tail. A dog wags his tail. But a hound waves his stern."

"I see," I say.

"And they don't bark."

"Hounds don't bark?"

"They give tongue."

I don't really know what to say.

"Language," says my host, "is as important to fox hunting as are dress and custom. Dress, custom, language, horses, foxes, hounds. They are the elements of the ritual." He seems to have drifted off into some reverie. I find myself thinking about Jack Russell.

"Sort of like a kangaroo?" I ask.

"What?" says my host.

"The riding groom carries Jack Russell in a pouch like a kangaroo."

"In fox hunting," he says, "there are not many comparatives."

"Only superlatives?"

"Exactly." There is another pause between us; the fire crackles. The party is closing in. Women begin moving among photographs of themselves on horses jumping over hedges and pretend not to notice themselves. Men, in not-quite-out-at-the-elbows tweed jackets, stand with what must be called "bearing" in groups of threes and fours and engage in comfortable conversation. Comfort. Theirs is a comfort not even Ralph Lauren can conjure.

"Tell me about 'tallyho,'" I urge.

Although I had not seen much of the hunt, I had in fact been startled to hear someone call out its most famous phrase; you don't really expect anyone in America to seriously say "tallyho" aloud, anymore than you'd expect to hear Nancy Reagan sing out, "Let them eat cake."

"Well," says my host, "there is all that rot about a French connection with 'tallyho,' and how it means 'out of the thicket a creature has run,' but it only means 'there's a fox.' Sort of like 'land ho!'"

"I don't suppose you could yell, 'There goes the [expletive] fox.'"

"That would not do," he says. "In fact, if you're a member of the field and see the fox, you should not say anything at all."

"What do you do, point?" Surely not, I thought. My mother always told me that in polite society you don't point. Dogs point, people do not. Probably hounds don't point either.

"Not exactly," my host says. "You stand your horse with his head toward the fox and take off your cap and hold it in the air. Soon someone on the hunt staff will see you and bring in the hounds. On the other hand, if a member of the hunt staff sees a fox, they should call out 'view holloa, view holloa, view holloa.' That call will bring the hounds."

"What's this about staff and field?" I say. Like all prairie populists, I suspect the East Coast is a barely latent class society.

"The hunt staff," my host says, "is made up of the master of the fox hounds, the huntsmen, the kennel men and the whippers-in."

"The whippers-in?" The phrase gives off a whiff of sadism, an attitude that I understand can arise in advanced societies.

"They control the hounds so they don't fan out too far. You want the hounds near the huntsmen. The main huntsman is the master of the foxhounds. He is, and here I think I can quote from Major Wadsworth's hunt bible, 'a great and mystic personage to be lowly, meekly and reverently looked up to, helped, considered and given the right of way at all times.' Do you see?"

"I see," I say. "And the field?"

"That's everybody who wants to watch the hunt," my host says.

"You mean most people on a fox hunt are just watching?"

"That's correct," he says. "If you want to get particular about it, the hunt is purely between the hounds and the fox. The huntsmen help the hounds chase the fox. The rest of us look on. Like other sports. Only our box seat is the back of a horse."

"Do you pay for your box seat" I ask. I hadn't intended to mention money; a friend of mine told me before I left for Middleburg that there is one subject you do not bring up (money) and one question you do not ask (What do you do for a living?).

"Of course," says my host with a wry smile. He seems to understand me in some way; I am grateful.

"How do you pay?" I ask. At least I didn't ask how much. "Well, not at the turnstile," he says, and laughs.

"I thought not."

"You subscribe to a hunt," he says. "It's like a club. Ours has 50 or so members. There are dues, and with the dues we hire the staff and care for the hounds."

"Then the master of the foxhounds is an employee?" I ask.

"That's so. 'The best of the servant class,' I heard one man remark."

"I thought that saying referred to teachers at private schools," I say.

"I've heard that as well," he says. We take more of our brandy. The women of the party are getting closer.

I remember in high school learning that at the beginning of the Civil War the society from Washington would travel out of the city to picnic in the meadows and watch a battle, perhaps before the evening's theater. I couldn't help but think some of them rather liked the lovely country in which the war was being fought and vowed to return when the one great silliness of our civilization was over. And was this what their return had come to? These lovely people at ease among themselves after an afternoon at sport. Not bad, if the choice is between a weary—or even a dead—fox and a torn nation. The world at any kind of play is better than the world at war; but of course the world is never so easily divided.

"Do you hunt all year?" I ask my host.

"No," he says. Then he sighs. "The season's over. From here on it is a long wait for cubbing."

"Cubbing?"

"That's when we train the hounds. And the fox."

"You *train* the fox?"

"Yes. To run. From the time they are young. The hunt staff does that. There's no field. The master goes out when the fox cubs are young and chases them until everybody gets the hang of it. It's a bit difficult to explain," he says, "but what it comes to is that we don't hunt all that much of the year so we want everyone to be in shape."

"Practice has its rewards," I say. Two women have come up to sit around the fire with us and be attractive. One has particularly lovely teeth.

"On the other hand," my host continues after brief introductions all around, "through the spring and summer we have our competitions. Steeplechase. Point-to-point. Trail rides. Dressage. It can all be quite stimulating, I suppose, even if it is not the real thing. The hunting, you see, is over."

Needless to say, just when we are trying to count the homeless in our nation's capital, putting your wrist against your forehead about the end of the fox-hunting season in The Plains, Warrenton, Winchester and other places pricey and princely is not the most popular of laments. He knows this. I know it. I change the subject.

"What's dressage?" I ask. As it happens, I have my own story about dressage.

"Well, it's one of the training sports," my host says. "For girls, mainly. The horses are brought into a ring and judged on quality of trot, quality of walks, transitions from one gait to another, quality of halt."

"It's quite lovely to watch," says one of the women. "Horse and rider perform a kind of ballet together."

"Quality of halt?" I ask.

"Halt," says my host, "is the most important gait in fox hunting."

"You mean 'whoa!'" I say. "As in 'Whoa! Dammit, horse, stop!'" The women stir slightly in their seats.

"'Halt' is the word," says my host. "We do a lot at halt waiting for the hunt staff. You are at halt when you raise your cap to say you've seen the fox. One book on the subject says if your horse won't stand, then shoot him."

"Horse meat is 50 cents a pound at the head chopper's barn in western Kansas," I say. The look I get from the women tells me I have said something out of place.

"All sports," says my host with some effort to continue, "such as steeplechase and dressage, have come from fox hunting."

"We thought dressage was a disease," I say.

"A disease?" says the woman with lovely teeth. The word has zipped shut her smile. "Why would you think that?"

"One day at a ranch where I once worked a lady stopped by in a Mercedes to ask if we boarded horses with dressage. I think now she must have said *for* dressage, but I heard it *with* dressage. That night at supper I told the rancher.

"'What's dressage?' he asked.

"'Maybe it's something a horse gets from being boarded in town,' I said.

"'We don't need that,' the rancher said. 'What if dressage gets into the grass from the horse shit and then into the cattle? We'd have every hamburger back yarder in six states getting dressage. Ralph Nader would trace it back here to Half Vast Ranch. The Vicky Vegetarians would be all over us like grasshoppers. What a mess.'"

My host laughs and stubs out his cigar. Even though horses

have gone lame crossing the pastures of misunderstanding between cowboy and fox hunter, I think my old ranch boss and my East Coast host might have gotten on after a fashion. Not that they would have swapped cigars. Or dogs.

"You do have to be careful about disease," says the woman with fine teeth; she and her friend excuse themselves and get up to circulate among the photographs of themselves and others.

"What about the steeplechase?" I ask after a moment.

"Once again, it's from the hunt," my host says.

"Where's the steeple?"

"On the church in an English village," he says. "Imagine it's after a hunt and you've still got some piss and vinegar in your horses. So you say to your friend, 'I'll bet my horse can beat your horse from here to there': and 'there' is the village church. Of course, in between are all kinds of brooks and logs and fences. That's why horses on the hunt have to be good jumpers. It started in Ireland, I think."

"And point-to-point?" I ask.

"Pretty much the same thing, only in point-to-point you race over what is called 'fair hunting country.' No woods and swamps in the way. These days, we just put up the barriers ourselves and race for prizes. We make a tour of it all. In general, all the races add up until you get to the Gold Cup steeplechases at Great Meadow in May."

"The Gold Cup?" I ask. It seems as if I've heard of that. Something social, I think.

"The Gold Cup," my host says. "It is our most celebrated event." He gets up and retrieves from a nearby desk the program of the Gold Cup's 60th running, in 1985. I leaf through it. It is rich with lists of patrons and small histories on thoroughbreds and steeple-chasing. The program accounts for seven races in all, with more than a hundred horses competing.

One of the riders is a woman named Marie Antoinette. For once, I decide to keep my mouth shut.

"I'll tell you what," my host says when he sees I've stopped reading. "Why not stay over and watch some races tomorrow? It will be great fun. I'll get you in. Be sure to watch the maiden race."

"The maiden race?"

"A race among horses who have never won."

"A race of losers?" I ask.

"It's never put that way," he says. "Instead, we say that when a horse wins, it has lost its maiden. There's something of life in the language of fox hunting."

"I see," I say.

"And horses are not 'bred.'"

"Immaculate conception?" I say.

I had noticed there were no cow flops in the pastures around Middleburg. Where I came from we are proud of our cow flops. A truck load of dried ones can still be heat on cold winter nights if times get really tough.

"When a mare is bred we say she has been 'covered.'"

"Discreet conception," I say.

"Quite." My host smiles. He pours me another brandy, and himself one as well. I thank him for his invitation to stay over and hope it can be arranged.

In fact, I do attend the maiden race the following day. You have the sense of being at a huge lawn party, a scene out of *The Great Gatsby* where all the guests—not just the one who is forever rooming in Gatsby's house—have stayed on until the morning after and the morning after that, for all the mornings of their lives. What else is there to do, these waking guests say, but saddle the horses, establish a course, have the help erect barriers here and there, fetch some pâté and Stilton and Chateau d'Ay, and settle in to watch the races. There is something of fox hunting in it all; and there is something of life itself in fox hunting. At least that is what the lovely lawn people will say to themselves in the checkered shade.

"And among the hunts," I say to my host as we rise from our

seats by the fire to rejoin the evening's party, "is one a better hunt than another? Is there that kind of competition?"

"All fox hunts are equal," he says, "but some are more equal than others." He smiles.

"And your hunt?"

"Very good," he says.

"Is there a better?"

"The Orange County Hunt is very good," he says.

"Why? The foxes? The horses? Famous people?"

"All of that," he says. "And civility as well. A good hunt is the sporting drama of civility."

"I see," I say.

It occurs to me that my host is a civil man. I say so. He nods.

I remember being taught that among the cultured people a sign of good manners is the ability to tolerate bad ones. With me around his house all weekend asking rube questions about money, and rattling on about dressage being a disease, and thinking that Jack Russell was married to Elizabeth Taylor, and hoping for a chance to tell my ranch jokes, it seems clear to me that my host has passed the test for which his rearing had trained him.

"Do you mind if I use your name in print? I ask. "When I write my story."

"Call me Deep Horse," he says.

"Deep Horse it is," I say.

"Would you like to know about 'drag'?" he says as we edge out into the glasses and dresses of the party.

"Yes," I say. "Tell me about 'drag.'"

"And have I told you why we 'bang' our tails?"

"You have not," I say.

"It is all quite amusing," he says.

"I see," I say.

"Spot"

The Family Dog

When I was a sophomore at the University of Kansas in the early '60s I spent a Christmas vacation taking the family dog to Africa. In those days my father worked for Trans World Airlines in Addis Ababa, Ethiopia. It fell to me to help pack up my mother and send her off before my fall semester classes began, then later, during my Christmas break, to follow with Pinocchio—our huge, aging, big-chested collie who in the meantime had stayed with relatives.

"What's that?" asked the airfreight man at the Kansas City airport.

"A crate for a dog," I said. A friend of mine with a pickup truck and I were off-loading a hand-built wooden dog kennel roughly the size of an old flying boxcar and about as heavy. It had chicken wire for windows and a built-in corner to hold a 10-pound sack of dog food. On the outside we had painted his nickname, "Pokey" (as a child I couldn't pronounce Pinocchio), and his destination: Box 1755, Addis Ababa, Ethiopia.

"What kind of dog?" the freight man asked. He seemed a little worried.

"A big dog," said my friend.

"He's friendly," I said.

"Let's hope," said the man.

Our plan was to bring Pinocchio to the airport later in the evening for the night cargo flight to New York. I was to follow the next morning and meet him for the trip to London and from there to Frankfurt, Athens, Cairo, Asmara and Addis Ababa.

Pinocchio *was* friendly. Well, he wasn't friendly toward the milkman who had tried to kick him. And once he trapped the water-meter-reading lady in the basement for hours by sitting at the top of the stairs and barking his deep, thundering bark. But at heart he was a gentle giant of a dog who no doubt would rather have spent his remaining days standing around a farmyard as if in a Hopper painting. That was not to be. We all had to get home for Christmas. And home was Northeast Africa.

"Have you seen a dog around here?" I asked a man at the freight headquarters in New York. My friend and I had successfully shipped Pinocchio the night before and I had made my morning flight with no problem. Since I was the son of an airline employee I was traveling on a pass and always had to-go space available—as did my dog. This required that I keep the two of us together by making sure we'd both make each flight. It's one thing to have you and your bags separated; it's another to get split up from the family pet.

"I guess we have," said the man in charge. "About the size of a crew bus."

"That's him," I said.

"Came in early this morning," the man said. "They've got him back in the hangar. He begs doughnuts."

Pokey was sleeping by the nose wheel of an old Lockheed Constellation.

"Has he been good?" I asked a cleaning woman working nearby.

"Real good," she said. "He probably needs a walk; we didn't think we should do that, but we thought it was all right to let him have the run of the hangar." She paused. "He begs doughnuts," she said.

"I'll bet he does," I said, and patted him. I attached his leash and we walked out onto the tarmac.

It was beginning to snow and I wondered if the evening flights to Europe would be taking off. Like most college kids, I traveled light and with little money; like most airline employees' kids I knew my way around the crew lounges of the major airports in the United States and Europe, so if we became stuck I could always camp out on a couch for a few days. The problem would be Pinocchio. My hope was a young man's trust in a worldwide Christmas Spirit.

The first hint of trouble came the next day. I happened to be standing in the doorway of the 707 we'd taken from New York to London, watching the planes from different countries come into Heathrow. In half an hour we were to make the short hop to Frankfurt where I'd have a day's layover waiting for the Ethiopian Airlines plane to come up from Athens.

We had been on one of the last flights out of Idlewild the night before; the whole East Coast was now closed in by a snowstorm. Boarding toward the end, I had waited until I was sure of a seat before I asked the freight handlers to load Pokey. Now in London I stood in the doorway and saw that the freight handlers were *unloading* him. In fact, they had brought out a special forklift to do the job. Down the stairs I raced.

"What's the matter'?" I asked. "That's my dog and he's supposed to go to Frankfurt. With me."

From the beginning I'd had a special fear of stopping in London. Everyone knows they don't take kindly to importing dogs, and in my imagination I could see the two of us quarantined for months on some barge parked in the Thames filled with dogs and owners who had misunderstood British laws.   .

"He comes off," said a burly Englishman. "Got to make room for some geese."

"Geese!" I said. By that time Pokey's crate had been hoisted high out of the belly of the airplane and I could see him eyeing the ground. My only hope was that no one would notice what he was until I could talk them into reloading him. That's when he started barking. Loudly.

"Geese for Christmas dinners at the military bases in Germany," said the Englishman.

"He won't hurt geese," I said. Pokey was still barking; he was stuck high in the air on that forklift and barking his head off and drawing a crowd.

"I guess he won't," said the Englishman. "Those geese are dead and plucked. It's just that there's a lorry of them. "

"What's the problem?" said the captain, who had seen me on the tarmac and come over.

"Don't think we got room for the dog," said the Englishman.

"I'm trying to get him home for Christmas," I said. The captain nodded.

"Keep the dog right here until you see what it looks like," he said. "Pack everything tight."

I went over to the forklift and called Pokey's name, and that calmed him. I could see him looking down at me and wagging his rump; the whole kennel wobbled.

I watched them load crate after crate of geese. Every time I thought they were finished, out would come another wagon with more. All the time I figured it was only a matter of moments before Pokey and I would be discovered by British bobbies and hauled off to the barge in the Thames.

"Put that dog aboard and close up," said the Englishman after inspecting the cargo hold as the last of the geese were being loaded.

"Thank you," I said.

"Sorry to put a fright in you," said the Englishman.

I didn't feel really safe until we started our roll down the runway for the leg to Frankfurt. Now began the slow part of the trip. Ethiopian Airlines didn't have jets in those days; they had DC-6Bs, and they flew into Frankfurt only three days a week. One of those planes—ET-26 it was called—had a cargo bay between the cock-pit and the passenger compartment where it was possible to carry a dog. I was to wait in Frankfurt until ET-26 made its run, then take it down to Athens and Addis. I might have to wait a few days for all this to work out. It was December 20, and the schedule could get tight.

The first night in Frankfurt I slept on a couch in the TWA freight office and Pokey slept on the floor beside me. The next day we went for a long walk into the country. The sun was out but it was cold. I watched my dog explore the German undergrowth and wondered if the smells he took in were much different from the smells of rabbits in Kansas. Then he spotted the swans.

We had come upon a park with a pond in it. There were some ducks and geese at one end, and a flock of white swans were sunning themselves high on a bank. Being a collie, Pinocchio was a herder. Once on a Boy Scout outing he had brought a small herd of steers into camp for us to admire; the farmer was not pleased. Now Pinocchio was determined to pin those swans into a corner.

Swans are not friendly birds. Nor, as it turns out, are they easily driven—even by a huge Kansas collie filled to the brim with the proper herding instinct. Back and forth he would go in front of the swans, barking and wagging his rump. The swans would flap their wings, dip their long necks down and out at him, and hiss. It was a standoff.

The racket brought a park guard, who said something to me I didn't understand.

"I don't speak German," I said. But I said it slowly and distinctly in the naive American assumption that by so doing I would make him understand me. Then he went over to where the swans were hissing and the dog was barking and began yelling. Absurdly, I realized that Pokey couldn't understand German either. Finally, the obvious occurred to me: I took out Pokey's leash and towed him off amid German profanity and the wing beats of highly agitated swans.

We walked back to the hangar to see if ET-26 had arrived. It had, but I could take it only as far as Athens where it would be loaded with cargo already piled up there. I *could* catch it when it made its run back up from Addis Ababa, which meant I would have to layover in Athens until the afternoon of the 23rd.

Athens was warm and it didn't seem like the holidays. I found a place for me and Pokey in the back offices of Ethiopian Airlines. The rooms were a jumble of packages and presents bound for the American radio base in Asmara as well as for the Americans stationed in Addis. Along a wall in one room were Christmas trees destined for Addis that had been flown down from Frankfurt over the previous weeks. Someone had brought in what looked like a long stock tank, filled it with water and stored the trees in it so they wouldn't dry out. Each tree had a tag with the owner's name on it. One of the trees was ours, and I had the sense I was gathering up parts of our American Christmas as I went along.

After we got settled I took Pokey for a long walk—on a leash this time—among the hangars and airport buildings. I was worried because he was running out of dog food and I was running out of money.

"Where do you want to go?" asked the man behind the TWA counter when I showed him my pass. I was going to have to leave Pokey in Athens while I made a food run.

"I'd like the flight to Rome and Paris," I said.

"That goes on to New York," he said. "Not going to Addis for Christmas? I see your dad is with EAL."

"Oh, I am," I said. "Just taking a small detour. I want to go up to Paris this morning and come back on the evening flight."

"You won't see much of Paris that way," said the man.

He was right, of course, but I wasn't flying to Paris to see it, I

ITINERARY
NINA R. HOUGHTON
March 27 – April 3, 2010

Saturday, March 27, 2010   To FL

9:30 am - David Stewart to pick up
Car: (410) 984-1679

Southwest # 1276 (2 hrs, 5 mins)
Economy, Confirm # Q7XHFL
Lv. BWI at 11:45 am
Ar. Jacksonville at 1:50 pm

Florida Residence

Saturday, April 3, 2010   To MD

Southwest # 2162 (1 hr, 55 mins)
Economy, Confirm # Q7XHFL
Lv. Jacksonville at 12:10 pm
Ar. BWI at 2:05 pm

David Stewart to drive home

was looking for a meal and some scraps for Pokey. Flying up I'd get a snack between Athens and Rome and I could save all of that. From Rome to Paris they'd serve lunch, and I'd save the rolls and crackers and fruit.

"Would you like some more rolls?" asked the hostess when she noticed mine were gone.

"Thank you," I said. "And another apple if you don't mind."

The return flight was another matter.

"It doesn't look good," the ticket agent in Paris said. I'd been afraid of that, but it was a chance I took. I had put out the rest of the dog food for Pokey as well as a bowl of water in his kennel in case I had to layover in Paris. One of the EAL baggage men said he'd walk him the following morning if I hadn't come back. I put Pokey in his kennel but the EAL people said they'd let him out after a while. Still, I was worried. You hate to leave your dog all alone like that with no one he knows around.

"Stand by," said the ticket agent in Paris. "We'll see how it turns out."

The crowd for the flight to Rome and Athens looked big. But, "We got one seat in first class," said the ticket man. "We're supposed to charge non-revs a service fee for first class," he added, "but why don't we skip that." I must have begun to look pretty seedy. My jacket pockets were beginning to bulge with the food I was hauling around. On the way down to Athens that night we had steaks in first class. I told the hostess about my dog and she filled a bag with all the leftovers from the other passengers, then she packed me a sack of bread and cheese.

"Merry Christmas," she said. "Good luck on the trip to Africa."

When I got back to Athens customs pulled me aside—all the food I was now carrying made me look so bulky they suspected I might be smuggling.

"Empty your pockets," a customs official said. He was nice about it. I laid all the cheese and bread and snacks on the table.

"What's in there?" he asked, pointing to the sack of leftover steak. "Scraps for my dog," I said.

"The big one at Ethiopian Airlines?" he asked.

"Yes," I said. "How did you know?"

"He got out this afternoon and wandered through the airport. Sent some people running, but made a few friends." He paused. "He begs."

"I know he does," I said. "Did he have any luck?"

"I saw him get an ice cream bar off a small boy," he said, "then someone took him back."

The customs man let me through and I found Pokey tethered to his kennel. He was glad to see me, although according to the EAL people he hadn't wanted for food. Nonetheless I fed him some of the steak scraps I'd collected and saved the rest for the next evening when we'd be taking ET-26 on the long ride to Addis Ababa. When the time came we—and the Christmas trees—boarded without incident The night flight to Cairo was smooth and we picked up a few passengers there but no cargo. I fed Pokey some more scraps and told him it wouldn't be long now. We left for Asmara in northern Ethiopia.

"They won't off-load the cargo compartment with the dog in there," said the captain on our arrival in Asmara. "We have to get him out."

It was about four in the morning. I had been asleep. I barely woke up when we landed, then drifted back to sleep until the captain came up.

"They think he's a lion," he said, "and they won't come on the plane. One guy did and he ran out yelling. Didn't you hear him?"

"No," I said. But I could hear Pokey barking in the front of the airplane. The passengers around me looked worried. When I walked up to the cargo bay I looked out the door. The ground crew had made a semicircle at the base of the aircraft. Some of them had climbed up on top of the baggage cart. There was quite a commotion. I got Pokey out of his kennel and took him down the steps. The ground crew fled.

"Get him way down the tarmac where they can't see him," ordered the captain. "Better yet, take him over the rainbow. I've got to get this plane loaded and out of here tonight if we're ever going to get home for Christmas."

Pokey and I took a long walk into the night. I could see the Asmara tower light flashing, and there were planes—now dark—from various airlines waiting to take off on morning flights. Looking back I could see the ground crew coming back to service ET-26. I knew we weren't to return until they left.

We waited at the edge of the darkness. "Good lion," I said to Pokey and patted him. He wagged his rump. "Good lion."

When we went back to the plane there was no one else around. I took Pokey up the flight of stairs and stowed him in his kennel. I fed him the rest of the scraps I'd saved from the Paris trip and the captain let me stay in the cockpit. In the east I could see the sun coming up over the desert below. I imagined there were men down there with camels, and I remembered my father telling me the Christians of Ethiopia—the Copts—were among the oldest Christian sects in the world. I wondered what they would think if they knew that 20-some thousand feet above them the airplane they heard was full of a younger world's celebration of Christmas: boxes of presents from England, trees from the German woods, and a large Kansas dog with an Italian name—all going home for Christmas.

"We've met the planes for the last few days," said my mother when we got to the airport at Addis Ababa. "We were concerned."

"You and Pokey didn't have any trouble, did you?" my father asked. I had let Pokey out of the crate and walked him down the aircraft's steps. He was glad to see everybody and wagged his rump and barked. He was beginning to draw a cautious crowd.

"None to speak of," I said. I had learned by then that it's best not to worry parents with the small details of adventure. Behind us they were unloading Christmas trees in the African sunlight.

The Radio Game

"See that graveyard over there?" says Ed Athey, athletic director of Washington College and head coach of the school's
baseball team. We are standing on the pitching mound of Kibler
Field in Chestertown, Maryland. This is more than twenty years
ago.

"Yes," I say. The graveyard toward which Ed is pointing shelves
itself on a hill behind the third base dugout and beyond the railroad tracks of the local grain train that cut through the back of
the college campus. It is out of reach of even the greatest slugger's drive: Not Swish Nicholson, not Home Run Baker, not
even Jimmie Foxx in his prime could have hit a pitch into the
Chestertown graveyard from where Ed and I are standing.

"What about it?" I say.

I am Ed Athey's new pitching coach, a volunteer from the faculty who has a modest career to his credit.

For the previous hour or so I have tried to relive ("revitalize"
is the word I really see in my mind's eye but I am keeping that
to myself) my baseball youth by hurling batting practice to the
lean and hungry hitters of the Washington College squad. It has
been slow going. My old form is no doubt somewhere in the
arrangement of the bones and muscles and cartilage of my bur-
geoning middle-aged body, but an afternoon of throwing has not

yet brought all these parts into anything like the dependable prose rhythm you need to pitch.

Two pitches in point: My curveball (which out of vanity—and I have noticed, to the barely contained amusement of the young hitters—I signal with a twist of the wrist before I throw so the catcher and batter know what's coming) has more the droop of a toothpick than the quick fishhook it needs to fool keen eyes. Eddie Lopat (who had three speeds of curve balls: slow, slower and slowest) is Bullet Bob Feller compared with me this afternoon. And my fastball—which even in my youth was never anything to point a radar gun at—seems to have lost what movement it once had, unless you count as "movement" a decided dropping off at about six feet six inches as if, approaching the end of a long day, it wanted to plop itself down on a couch for a nap.

Beyond these two staples in my repertoire I have tried my Hoyt Wilhelm knuckleball (in the dirt five out of five times, although one batter hit it on the bounce for a clean single to right); my Ewell Blackwell sidearm cross-fire (thrown about a foot behind a startled right handed hitter: two out of two times); my change-up (telegraphed so clearly that it looked like Satchel Paige's "hesitation" pitch: two shots, both out of the park); a Christy Mathewson "fadeaway," the ancient version of a "screwball" (hit over the left field fence two out of five times); two sliders (no slide, no drop, nadda: deep doubles); two spitballs (one resulting in a clothesline drive down the third base line and one in a rifle shot back through the box that made me feel like Herb Score when Gil McDougald took aim); and finally some Walter "Big Train" Johnson semi-submarine pitches, most of them hitting high on the backstop and dropping to the ground like dead pigeons. In this version of my "revitalization" I begin to see myself as some slow-pitch softball moundsman sent onto the field by Bill Veeck to bring comic relief to an otherwise dull game. Call me Eddie Gaedel. Ah, the stages of life.

"There are arms in that graveyard," says Coach Athey, giving me a wan smile and a pat on the back because Ed can no more be cross with a man than he can tell a story that isn't true, "there are arms in that graveyard that have more life in them than yours."

Truth is a fastball high and tight that backs you out of the box every time.

EASTERN SHORE LEAGUE, THEN AND NOW
The Eastern Shore of Maryland was once wonderful baseball country. If you believe in ghosts, or in the real live Ed Athey who retired as athletic director a few years back but still coaches the Washington College team—it still is. The truth of my dead arm is another matter.

From about 1922 until 1949, the towns that sprawl along or near the coves and creeks and estuaries on this side of Chesapeake Bay fielded a number of Class D minor league teams. In Maryland, Crisfield and Salisbury and Cambridge and Easton and Pocomoke City all had teams at one time or another. In Virginia, teams represented Parksley and Northampton County; while in Delaware, Dover and Laurel, among others, put players destined for the major leagues onto the field. "Shore hopes," I believe these players considered themselves. And Shore hopes might well have been what their fans thought they were cheering.

Most of the ballplayers on these teams were not home-grown. They shagged flies and fielded grounders and doubled to left among the soybean fields and the peach groves and the cantaloupe patches long enough to ripen for the big leagues: strangers in the land of pleasant living. Mickey Cochrane (Athletics and Tigers, catcher), Joe Collins (Yankees, first baseman), Carl "The Reading Rifle" Furino (Dodgers, outfielder), Danny Murtaugh (Pirates, second base and manager), Red Ruffing (Red Sox, Yankees, pitcher), George "Twinkletoes" Selkirk (Yankees, outfielder) and Mickey Vernon (Senators, first baseman) all once saw action on the Eastern Shore. At least two major league umpires (Larry Napp and Frank Dascoll) called balls and strikes in such towns as Centreville, Maryland and Milford, Delaware. Connie Mack himself once served as president of the Federalsburg A's. But most of the Eastern Shore League's national fame comes from strictly local heroes.

Driving into Sudlersville, Maryland., from Church Hill, Maryland, along Route 300, you cross Dell Foxx Road. Note the two xs in Foxx, the same two employed by James Emory, "Double X" Foxx, the author of 534 career home runs and a .325 lifetime batting average. Dell Foxx—or Mr. Dell, as he was called—was Jimmie Foxx's father. While Dell Foxx Road is a memorial to the farm family that reared the great Athletics and Red Sox slugger, a large engraved stone in the center of Sudlersville is the town's tribute to the hitter himself.

Not far away in Chestertown, near the town hall, is a statue in honor of Bill "Swish" Nicholson (all-star outfielder for the Cubs and still very much alive, thank you), his bat finishing a swing that has no doubt hit one clear into the Chester River, three blocks away. The nickname, by the way, came from what Ed Athey calls the "emphatic" swing Nicholson had.

"If he missed a pitch, you could hear his bat cutting the air ," says Ed. "When he came up to the plate the fans would cheer, 'Swish, Swish, Swish.' It would go around the stands like a wave." As for Frank "Home Run" Baker of Trappe, Md., he got his name when—as a third baseman for Connie Mack's Philadelphia Athletics—he pounded a game-tying homer against Christy Mathewson (the Prince of Pitchers) of John McGraw's New York Giants. It was in the third game of the 1911 World Series, and while Home Run Baker led the National League that season and the three seasons after that, he did so—in that pre-Ruthian era—by hitting a dozen or fewer home runs a year.

THE RADIO. CIRCA 1950

By stringing a few extension cords together I could get my father's basement radio (a pre-portable model) halfway down the gravel driveway that abutted the dirt road that ran by our house.

On the other side of the road were a vacant yard to the north-west (right field) and an abandoned house to the southwest (left field). Deep center (due west) was the remains of a back yard picket fence. Home plate was the end of our driveway. Balls were rocks from the driveway, while my bats were a series of "hitting sticks" I would fashion out of scraps from father's carpentry projects. The ball game itself (in which I was always the batter) would be dictated by the Saturday or Sunday afternoon radio broadcast of the out-of-town-games played by the Kansas City Blues, a Triple-A farm team for the New York Yankees. Although the three-person Day family lived deep into the country west of Kansas City, I was—as it turned out—not a boy too far from town to learn baseball.

Cerv hits a drive deep to left-back, back, back. It is going. It is going. It's gone. It is over the fence. A two-run homer for Bob Cerv with Bill Renna scoring in front of him. What a drive, folks. What a drive. Out of sight!

As Bill Renna had already singled sharply to center with a rock shot over the road and into the grass just beyond the drain-age ditch, it was only a matter of putting Bob Cerv's homer over the roof of the vacant house (on the roof was a triple; against the wall was a double), something I could usually do before the next batter came up, but not without a few foul balls and a couple of ground-ers that didn't count in the game of my dreams. Sooner or later there would be that solid whack of my hitting stick against a good round rock, and off Cerv's drive would go in perfect imitation of what happened on the radio.

What my father thought of all this as he sat in a lawn chair reading the sports page and listening to the ball game he never said, although surely he must have noted there was some pace to my hitting stones that matched the play-by-play on the radio. Also, it was our custom in those days to play a game of catch after the "radio game"—as he called it—was over. Throwing the ball back and forth, my father would from time to time toss me a "grounder" to one side or the other, and if I fielded it well he'd say: *That's a Phil Rizzuto for you. That's a Pee Wee Reese.*

On fly balls I'd be Joe DiMaggio or, because my father was a Red Sox fan, due to his deep admiration for Ted Willlams's service in the Korean War, I would become, when I caught up with one of his tossed deep drives, a Dom DiMaggio. *That's a Dom DiMaggio. Do you know who Dom DiMaggio is?*

As Dom DiMaggio was not on the radio in Kansas City, I did not. *He's the forgotten brother of Joe, just like Korea will be the forgotten war*, my father would say. *Don't forget the forgotten.*

If I muffed the grounder or dropped the long fly, my father would throw one in just the same place—and he would do this until I fielded it correctly. In this way all my errors on our front lawn cum Kansas City Blues fantasy baseball field were swept clean, so that my play seemed as spotless as a new uniform or a freshly dusted home plate.

But while my father indulged me (and perhaps himself) in our imitation baseball games, it is true as well that he was the one who, a few summers later (it was the same summer we discussed—in a roundabout way—the origin of puppies), broke the bubble of illusion about radio games and told me that the out-of-town baseball I was listening to on these Saturday and Sunday afternoons was broadcast not from, say, Minneapolis, where the games were in fact being played, but from a building in Kansas City, complete with prerecorded crowd noise and bat whacks.

The announcers, my father asserted, were describing the Bob Cervs and the Cliff Mapeses and Ralph Houks from a ticker tape they were getting in the studio near the radio tower that I could see at night out of my bedroom window blinking, blinking in the distance, 20 or so miles to the east.

I remember my hitting stick was in my hand when my father told me the true nature of the radio baseball broadcasts. Mickey Mantle (who had been sent to the minors briefly by the Yankees) had just doubled to right. A double to right was tricky business on my field. You had to put it between a cottonwood tree in right center and a dead ash tree that marked the right field foul line and in which a mother blue jay was raising her young. Beyond that, you had to hit a pile of rubble that was an abandoned car and various other metal junk, which would ping to signal your two-base hit. Before I pitched up my stone for my left-handed swing (like Mantle, I could hit from both sides of the plate), I hesitated. What was I hitting? Was it a stone or a ball? *Next up is the catcher*... Where was I hitting it? Into the right field fence or into a pile of Studebaker rubble? Who was on first? Was that Ralph Houk coming up or Bobby Day? What was the score? Who was I? *What's the matter, son?* Not a thing, I think now, as long as I can imagine the game for myself. Television, I have learned, is the real enemy of reality.

HOME RUN BAKER, 1995

"I once met Frank Baker," Ed Athey says to me. We are sitting in the third base dugout at Kibler Field on the Washington College campus. This is just a few weeks ago. The college team has not yet come out for practice. The day is warm. The dogwoods are in full bloom; the campus lilac bushes are beginning to blush. The infield grass is clipped and the base paths have been freshly dragged. The pitcher's mound looks lonely without me. I have come to ask for my old job back but worry I won't have the nerve.

Tom Kibler (for whom the field is named) was Ed Athey's coach, and once president of the Eastern Shore League. Kibler and Home Run Baker had played ball together. The history of baseball is, like most histories, linked to the past by a series of serendipitous handshakes. I am about to learn that the man whose hand I shook by way of greeting earlier this afternoon has shaken the hand of Home Run Baker, who in his turn no doubt shook hands with Walter Johnson, into whose glove William Howard Taft (the first president to throw out an opening day ball) once tossed a slow fat one at the Washington Senators' National Park (at Seventh and Florida NW) to start the 1910 season.

"What was he like?" I say. "Home Run Baker. What was he like?"

"Big," says Ed. "I remember thinking when he came out of his home in Trappe, 'That's a big, rawboned man.' He had a ruddy out-door quality to him. He might have been a farmer who worked in the fields all day, he looked so strong and healthy. I can see his face now. Stern. Like he was still trying to get a hit."

"Did you talk baseball?"

"He talked baseball with Coach Kibler," says Ed. "We were giving Baker a ride to Salisbury for an award by the Eastern Shore League. I sat in the back seat all the way down and all the way back, but I sat forward in it and right in the middle so I could hear everything they said. They talked about home runs and about how soft the ball was when Frank Baker played. He seemed to remember one home run in particular. I think it was toward the end of his career."

"Did you ever see Ruth play?" I ask.

"I did," says Ed Athey. "I saw him on a barnstorming tour over in Cumberland, Maryland. He was playing in the Wineow Street stadium. He was with a whole team of major leaguers whose names you could find in any baseball book today, but I can't remember anybody but Ruth. You knew him the minute you saw him. He filled the field."

"Did he homer?"

"He did. And it was the longest home run he ever hit."

"How do they know?" I ask.

"Because it went over the right field fence and landed in a coal car that was passing through on the tracks that ran just outside the stadium. The ball probably went another hundred miles before it touched ground." Here Ed laughs in delight at the story.

"Did you see it land in the coal car?" I ask.

"I did not." says Ed. "I was sitting too low in the stands to see the trains go by the outfield fence. I could hear them, though. But you had to sit up higher to see Ruth's homer land in the train. Somebody told me that's what happened. I don't even know if it's true."

"I would have seen it," I say. "No matter where I had been sitting. I can see it now. It bounces once when it hits the coal and raises a puff of dust."

"That's why you're a writer," says Ed.

THE AUTHOR, 1950

The summer I was eight, my father took me down to the Cub Scout ballpark for the tryouts. That would be the year I started playing baseball for real instead of just in the radio games I banged out at the end of my driveway (although those would continue for many years).

"What position do you want to play?" my father asked as we were driving to the field.

"Batter," I said.

"Everybody's a batter," he said. "You have to play some other position."

"I just want to bat," I said. "I don't want to play another position." This was all before television and before I had ever seen a real game of baseball. Hearing games over the radio and playing catch with my father, I of course understood in some dim way that there were players other than batters.

"You play in the field for half an inning and then you bat for the other," he said.

"I don't want to," I said. What parents never seem to understand about children is how much their world is shaped by themselves. And how little of it they are willing to explain by way of explanation: How to tell my father that only batters mattered because in the game at the end of the driveway (which was the only game going in my mind), I was always the batter. And I was all batters just as he was all fathers. How to be other than ourselves?

"We'll see," said my father.

What we saw (what I saw) was that the game as played on a field other than my own had as its author a player who stood on a mound of brown dirt with a white dash running partway across it—and that I wanted to be that author. Did I think that then? I must have: I think it now. How else to explain that puff of coal dust rising from Ruth's home run?

THE BALL, CIRCA 1990

A number of years ago, Amos, my Labrador retriever, made the national news for his ability to sniff out and retrieve all kinds of lost balls in the raspberry and blackberry patches that border the athletic fields at Washington College. Mainly he retrieved lacrosse balls, nearly a thousand over a 10-year stretch. But he also found softballs (10), soccer balls (two—he pushed them out of the weeds with his nose) and baseballs (a hundred or so). One of those baseballs was an especially old and black one with its cover badly torn so that you could see the string inside. I saved it to give to Ed Athey at a celebration in his honor when he retired as athletic director.

"I have in my hand," I said when it came my turn to speak, "the last ball Ed ever hit out of the park at Kibler Field as a player for Washington College. That was on June 4th, 1942, at 2:32 in the afternoon. Amos retrieved it just this week. It was buried so deep in the weeds it took him an hour to dig it out." There was some general laughter and a round of applause.

"That dog saved us a lot of money over the years," said Ed, looking at the beaten-up old ball I had just given him. "And we sure are grateful," he went on, now beginning to turn the ball around in his hand as if studying a lineup card. "But I have to say, I don't think this is the last ball I hit out. I think I went and got that one back myself."

In my mind's eye, I am throwing the pitch Ed hit: It is my Ewell Blackwell sidearm cross-fire, this time with a screwball tacked onto the end so that after it drives Ed out of the box, it sneaks back over the plate for a strike. But the pitch is so slow that Ed can recover before it slips into the catcher's mitt. He belts it halfway to the graveyard. Somewhere I hear the whistle of a coal train coming down the tracks.

SORRENTO, ITALY, CIRCA 1951

I am standing at the end of a jetty that goes out into the Mediterranean. I have found myself an Italian hitting stick, a smooth piece of driftwood. With it I am hitting line drives and towering home runs into the water. Center field is Sardinia, right field is Corsica and left field is Capri (we have been studying world geography in grade school, and one of the conditions my parents have placed on me during this—our first trip to Europe—is that I know both where I am and where I have been).

Where I have been during the previous hour is hitting stones into the sea while my mother and father amble the streets and poke among the shops of Sorrento itself. (My father, by the way, in Rome the previous day, has sung "Come Back to Sorrento" to my mother at Alfredo's restaurant in his fine Irish tenor voice and to the complete amazement and no doubt embarrassment of Alfredo's American tourist patrons, but to the great delight of the Italian waiters—and of Alfredo himself, who has given my mother the pasta bowl out of which he has dispensed his fettuccine).

It is nearly sundown as I make my way toward the end of the game. Yogi Berra (the Kansas City Blues have given way to the 1953 New York Yankees, and without a radio I am playing my own games in my own mind) has just singled toward the coast of France. Cannes, no doubt. Hank Bauer (who doubled toward Tunis) has come home.

About half an hour before I have noticed some small boys playing soccer on the beach. Now they are coming up the jetty, keeping their ball in front of them with their feet. My hitting is about to draw a crowd, albeit a tiny one, and of course one that will have to cheer me on in Italian.

Giving up Gene Woodling (he hits sixth in my lineup) for some general outfield fungos, I rap a few flies into the water. A boy kicks the soccer ball gently in my direction.

I put my foot out to stop it, but it rolls past me. Everybody laughs.

The boy who kicked me the ball makes a waving motion with his arm, something like hitting. I give him my bat, pick up a few stones from the jetty and give them to him as well. He looks at me for a moment, then tosses one tentatively in the air, swings, and misses. He tries again: no luck. I don't feel so bad about the soccer ball. Five strikes later, he pops up. In my mind's eye Billy Martin catches it with ease around second base.

"DiMaggio," he says to me as he gives me back the bat. I give him his soccer ball, which I have picked up. "DiMaggio," he says again, pointing at me.

"DiMaggio," says one of the boys from the group there on the jetty. They all point at me. "DiMaggio."

I pick up some stones, sorting through them to find good round ones. Facing the sea, I open my stance in imitation of the Yankee Clipper, even though he is not on my team.

"DiMaggio," I say.

"DiMaggio," they say.

I toss up my best stone and hit a towering drive well over Andy Patko in left field and into the bleachers of Alexandria. Grace under pressure. Everybody cheers.

THE STRETCH, NOW AND THEN—AND IN THE FUTURE

Probably more than half of the text of baseball writing is statistics. Readers of *The Sports Encyclopedia of Baseball (Expanded, Revised and Updated)*, Grosset and Dunlap, 1981 (it's the most recent edition I have), will find a hundred pages of statistics for every page of prose. (Sloppy Thurston on Page 141, for example, was a right-handed pitcher for the Chicago White Sox in 1924, was at that time 25 years old. Among his other 13 statistical accomplishments, he pitched one shutout and had an earned run average of 3.80. There is not mention of origin of his first name.) In baseball, immortality in print is a matter of lines in the tables, not volumes on the shelf—much less home runs that land in coal cars or on the beaches of Corsica. Put another way, baseball statistics are the ultimate factual prose, the epitome of nonfiction. Truth itself. Ah, truth.

My own statistical life is more dubious, mainly because I am the author of it both on the field and off: in the book and out. Full disclosure here: Everything I have written thus far is true the way radio baseball is true, including the following table:

Player: Day, Robert.

Position: Batter (1950-1950); Pitcher (1950 to present); Writer (1950 to present).

Teams: Kansas City Radios (1949 to present); New York Yankees (1953 to present);

Sorrento All Stars (1953 to present); Washington College Sho'men (1972 to present).

Won/Lost: Yes.

THE BALL, 1953-1995

There is a baseball on the desk where I write. It has the autographs of the 1953 Yankees: Allie Reynolds, Ewell Blackwell, Mickey Mantle, Phil Rizzuto, Casey Stengel, Larry Berra, Hank Bauer, Vic Raschi, Gil McDougald, Frank Crosetti, among others. Like some writers I know who touch wood to keep their game going, I touch the ball to coach my paragraphs around the bases. It is my hope that the signatures will not fade before I do.

My father and I bought the ball from a vendor (it was the last in his case) in Yankee Stadium one Sunday afternoon: two dollars from my father's wallet and all three dollars from a roll of one-dollar bills bound tightly by a rubber band and kept in my right front jeans pocket. It was what was left of the five dollars I had brought as my allowance all the way from Kansas City to New York.

We had seen the balls for sale on the way in—or at least I had. All through the game (which Vic Raschi pitched and the Yankees won) I remembered those balls: They filled up the field in my mind even as the players who had signed them filled the field in front of me.

Between innings four and five my father and I left our seats to get some peanuts, and I went one stall down to look again at the balls, now much fewer in number. During the seventh-inning stretch, I went on my own to the men's room and stopped by the ball vendor to look once again. He was down to two balls. He pulled one out of the case and put it on the counter. I could see that Phil Rizzuto had signed just beneath Ray Scarborough. I touched my three dollars in my pocket and wished I had five.

After the game, my father led me to the vendor who had the baseballs. There was one left.

"You want to sell the boy that ball," my father said.

"He's been looking at it," said the man as he took the ball out of the case and spun it around on the top of the counter, then tossed it to me. "Do you throw your fastball with the seams or across them?" he asked.

"Across them," I said, putting my index finger and middle finger across Tom Gorman and Casey Stengel.

"You'll get better movement with the seams," said the man.

"How much?" said my father. Maybe he was hoping for a sale price at the end of the game.

"Five dollars." said the man. "Five dollars and he'll never forget it. Cheap for a memory." He was right about that.

THE WINDUP. 1995

"You don't need a batting practice pitcher this year, do you?" I say in such a way that Ed Athey won't think I'm serious. His players are coming out from the locker room for practice. Some of them are beginning to toss the ball around. The mound looks lonely without me.

Ed gets up and we step outside the dugout. He points over the roof toward where the train tracks cut through the back half of the campus. The coal train has passed taking Babe Ruth's homer with it. Behind us I can hear the swish, swish of two strikes, then the thump of a drive hit into the Chester River. I see myself catching the opening day pitch from President Taft, the 1953 Yankees gathered on the field behind me. In the first inning Berra will hit a double into an abandoned Studebaker in right. Mantle will follow with a long drive in the direction of Tunis.

"You see that graveyard?" Ed says.

"There are arms over there," I say, "that..." Writers always get to throw the final pitch.

High Plains Drifter

I am sitting by myself in one of the theater seats that line the tin-roofed boardwalk of Gove, Kansas waiting for my friend Fred Whitehead to drive *Squirrel Tooth* (that's the name of his pickup) back from Dodge City, 100 miles to the south.

Gove's picture-show business went belly up a number of years ago and—so they hauled the seats outside in order to give the dusty ranchers of western Kansas a place to plop down and gripe about government and politics after they've picked up a few supplies at the only store in town: beans, bureaucrats, rice, Perot, pickled eggs, Gennifer Flowers, Spam, Pat Buchanan and beef jerky.

Today—a Saturday—the store for some reason is closed. A note of explanation has blown off its thumbtack and flounces up and down the boardwalk. All around me the Indian summer of the Great Plains is beginning to settle in like so many yellow cottonwood leaves filling up the bar ditches and pheasant draws of the country. Every now and then a pickup with a stock rack in back comes down the road carrying a sorry steer or an old smooth mouthed gelding. It's a sale-barn day nearby, and the head choppers from Denver or Kansas City are licking their pencils. But mainly this country is empty: Gove's version of "The Last Picture Show" doesn't have Timothy Bottoms sweeping the street, much less Cybill Shepherd unhooking her bra before she dives into a plush private pool. The High Plains may be the big picture, but like the theater I'm sitting in front of, it's largely a vacant one. The old gelding whinnies off-screen heading out of town. A cock pheasant cackles just before the whir of his flight.

"I'm going back to Dodge," Fred had said to me this morning. We were driving south out of Quinter toward Castle Rock, a range of monument rocks that bolt up out of otherwise flat cattle pastures like heads of "Star Wars" creatures. Given Kansas's reputation for table-top geography, travelers who see the Castle Rock formations for the first time (or the Chalk Pyramids farther west) must wonder—not unlike Dorothy to Toto—where they are anymore.

As for the two of us, Fred and I have been making something of an annual pilgrimage around the Kansas-Nebraska stretch of the Great Plains for a number of years now. I think—and perhaps Fred does as well—that we are looking for something on these trips, but we are not quite sure what. We don't talk about it in any direct way. Sometimes—like the year we went to the rainmakers' convention in Colby, Kansas (it didn't rain)—we know exactly where we are going. This year is different. We've been driving Fred's old gray Dodge pickup in no particular straight line for about a week now: Fort Wallace, the Chalk Pyramids, Fort Hays, Dodge City, Pawnee Rock, Fort Larned and Herndon in Kansas, Ogallala and Paxton in Nebraska. Finally, two days ago, we drove into Quinter for a buffalo-meat meal at the Q Inn Restaurant (Fred took a bowl of buffalo chili and I had the buffalo K.C. strip; we couldn't spend $20 between us) and a night in the adjacent motel. Our plan called for one more look at Castle Rock the next day before driving Interstate 70 back to Kansas City.

But Fred is given to changes. He is like the weather out here: steady for a long time with periods of uncertainty, cells of green-black hail on a prairie of sunshine, streamers of light among tornado clouds. But then his change of plans may be less about his being mercurial and more a reflection of his desire to have one more shot at finding whatever it is he seeks on trips such as these. It doesn't matter to me. I could ride shotgun forever.

"Why?" I asked. We had been in Dodge earlier in the week, spending a couple of days prowling through the museums and walking the historic streets. It's a good and bad town these days: half tourist trap with staged gunfights for the Japanese, and half old cow town full of the real ghosts of a real past. You need to know where to look. If you do, it's worth it.

"I forgot the Santa Fe train depot," Fred said. "My WPA guide notes two big rock sundials. One set on Central time, one on Mountain time. That's where the trains changed their clocks. I keep meaning to look at them."

That's probably less than half of it. Politically, Fred comes close to being a radical prairie populist and as such (and as editor of the respected anthology *Free-Thought on the American Frontier),* he's one of the few custodians of that largely forgotten tradition of western history. Ask Fred about the 19th-century West and you don't get John Wayne in a John Ford movie (much less Doris Day as Calamity Jane or Elizabeth Taylor as Poker Alice), you get Mysterious Dave Mather and the time he fired off a few rounds over the heads of the "she pillars" and the "he pillars" in a Dodge City church. Fred probably wanted to go back to Dodge to look for the bullet holes—or at least to stand on the spot where it happened and laugh to himself about how the *gunfire* ran the pious preacher out of town.

"Leave me off at Gove," I said.

"To sit in the movie seats," Fred said.

"Yes."

"You sure?" he said.

"I'll watch the shadows get fat," I said.

We have split the sheets this way before. It is as if Fred and I were a couple of old bulls too independent to be driven in a straight line, much less in a herd. The men of *Lonesome Dove* would have left us behind at Horsehead Crossing in south Texas. Fair enough if you've got hundreds of steers, two pigs and a "two-dollar-a-poke" woman-of-price to get to Montana before it snows. But Fred and I—with no last cattle drive to make—have our own methods of traveling the High Plains: I call his "historical gunkholing." He's always looking for places *where* something happened, preferably something obscure with irony to it. That's why Fred's main navigational bibles are the old Depression era guidebooks commissioned by the Work Projects Administration, which he's picked up at used book shops and which are complete with late-1930s maps tucked in the back. Thanks to his reading from these books, there are days when I think I know more about Alf Landon's Kansas than about Bob Dole's Kansas.

From his side of the truck, Fred calls my way of road riding "windshield wish booking." On these trips I like nothing better than to stare out windows at the sweep of prairie and look at the red tail hawks, the limestone fence posts, or at the occasional coyote slipping through the short-grass pastures in search of a jackrabbit. Windmills on a hill against a mounting thunderhead, or an old mottled longhorn looking at me from a rattlesnake pasture: That's my kind of scenery. I like as well to look down the half-deserted streets of broken towns that have "Closed by FDIC" spray-painted on the bank's window. Often there are davenports and easy chairs still on the front porches of abandoned houses, as if ready for a summer evening should times change and the town folk—who not all that long ago left for Denver or Los Angeles—return home with stories to tell about traffic in the big city and how you can hear gunfire after the sun goes down.

What I'm looking for out my side of *Squirrel Tooth*, I'm not sure—no more, I suspect, than is Fred when he peers into the V of his WPA guides. I do know that my idea is to store such scenes of plains desolation in a home movie of memory so that later I'll be able to watch it in my mind's eye. It's "wish booking" of sorts, Fred's right about that. This trip—now that I run it back from my Gove theater seat—has been more montage than narrative; more muted than technicolor; plotless and open. Less Victor Fleming and more Robert Altman.

DODGE CITY, KANSAS

We got to Dodge via Coffeyville down near the Oklahoma border. Coffeyville was the home town of the Dalton gang and the site of its most famous (and final) bank robbery. It was also—almost as important from Fred's point of view—the occasion for a witty passage from his WPA guide, which he read to me (he usually does this by holding the book open on the steering wheel as we go along, which produces a wobble to old Squirrel Tooth that must look like first-class drunk driving) as we drove into town:

> "When the firing broke out, rheumatic old men who had hobbled with difficulty a moment before dived into convenient barrels with acrobatic agility. Pedestrians crawled headfirst under culverts and remained there trembling, unmindful of protruding hindquarters. Men of wide girth squeezed behind thin hitching posts. "I have to admit," I said, "it's not the kind of prose you find in the Michelin Green Guide to the Popes' Palace in Avignon."

"It's not the kind of prose you find by any government writer these days," Fred said. "Even Peggy Noonan." Fred can be especially mean-spirited about late 20th-century political discourse.

After an hour or so in Coffeyville, we headed northwest to catch the old Santa Fe Trail at Fort Larned, stopping just east of there to study the enormous limestone Pawnee Rock, from which, Fred told me, one traveler on the Santa Fe Trail estimated he saw a herd of buffalo the size of Rhode Island. Don't get Fred started on the slaughter of the buffalo or what the federal government did to the Plains Indians. We left for Dodge, pretty much following the Santa Fe Trail.

Although Larry McMurtry doesn't let his *Lonesome Dove* cowboys spend very much time in Dodge City, they were probably the only ones on the 19th-century cattle trails who didn't. One measure of rough men's presence in Dodge was that by the 1880s so many women-of-price had flocked to Dodge they were called "doves," and their places of business "roosts." The High Plainsman always loves verbal irony especially with a poker face.

Dodge was all the time being shot up by both buffalo hunters and cowboys (the former were in fact the nastier of the two fraternities). With herds of up to 40,000 Texas longhorns pastured to the south (on the plains in summer the wind blows from that direction), plus buffalo hides piled by the railhead (a Tom Nixon once killed 120 buffalo in 40 minutes west of town), and with the dead and drunk cowboys spread-eagle in the streets, Dodge must have smelled like a toxic waste dump. It probably was. But of course great history is made in messy places like Dodge City, and it is its history that Dodge City sells today.

History and "Gunsmoke" television. Nothing is the same after you take a picture of it, and Dodge City is no exception. The old part of Dodge had partly fallen down and partly burned down by the early years of the 20th century. Its beam-and-board outfitting stores and whorehouses and taverns were rebuilt as settlers' stores in the sturdy post-Carry Nation merchant-class brick that survives today. But when "Gunsmoke" galloped into America's living rooms in the 1950s, life imitated art and Dodge City renamed its streets for gunfighters (Wyatt Earp Boulevard) and built itself a theme park, Old Dodge City, complete with Dodge City Days. (Part of the replica burned down again this past summer, again because of a gunfight: One of the actors shot into a moneybag, and a spark smoldered, then burst into flame, after the props had been stored for the night.)

Fred and I didn't bother with Old Dodge City, as neither of us are fans of pathetic irony. Instead we spent a pleasant hour or so in the restored Carnegie Center for the Arts on the corner of Second and Spruce, and later in the Kansas Heritage Center, housed at 1000 Second Ave., where there was a small exhibition of photographs of early Dodge and a pile of books and maps on the Old West, including a fine reproduction of Michael H. Bevans's map, "America and the Buffalo," done in the 1950s, and in itself an excellent historical narrative of the American bison.

"We could never find Mr. Bevans," said a clerk at the Heritage Center. "So we have to reprint his map without his permission. We thought it an educational service so people could understand what happened to the buffalo. We hope Mr. Bevans won't mind, considering. I hope he stops by someday. We probably owe him."

Back outside, Fred took me on a walking tour of the real Dodge complete with references not only to his beloved WPA guide, but also to Fredric R. Young's *Dodge City* and Nyle H. Miller and Joseph W. Snell's *Great Gunfighters of the Kansas Cowtowns, 1867-1886.* If Fred is a good example, then a little reading will go a long way to getting the pap of Matt Dillon and Miss Kitty out of your imagination; instead you'll see the real wild men and women of Dodge: Squirrel Tooth Alice (for whom I've named Fred's truck), Dog Kelley (once the mayor), Brick Bond (a druggist selling wines and whiskeys for "medicinal, mechanical and scientific purposes"), and Big Nose Katie Elder (a "friend" of Doc Holliday's). How'd you like to run for public office these days with "friends" like those to answer for? Not that the 19th-century press was kind to Dodge City. Even tough Texas cowboys the likes of the *Lonesome Dove* men were warned off: "Dodge has many characteristics which prevent its being classed as a town of strictly moral ideas and principles," lamented the *Corpus Christi Gazette*. "…Fast men and fast women are around by the score, seeking whom they may devour, and many is the Texas cowboy who can testify as to their ability." And even the *Washington Times* of the day was shocked (shocked!) at what went on in pre-Eisenhower Kansas: "Dodge City is a wicked little town…The Texas cattle drovers…loiter and dissipate sometimes for months, and share the boughten dalliances of fallen women." Lectures from Washington about family values are nothing new, it seems.

For our part, both Fred and I lament the demise of the old Lora Locke Hotel. It was a great place to spend a night. Situated on Gunsmoke Street, the hotel had plopped its restaurant down in the lobby so you ate artery-clogging steaks while watching cattle buyers register at the desk. The hotel itself had seven or so stories of straight-talking single-shot rooms but only one suite: the Willard Scott Suite.

"We heard he was coming to Dodge and wanted a 'suite of rooms,'" said the woman who used to clerk at the reception desk when I asked about it a number of years ago. I remember she had a beehive hairdo the size of a thunderhead.

"We didn't know quite what a 'suite of rooms' was," she said, "but we knew it had to be big because to look at him on television, Willard's big. Fills up the whole screen." To create a "suite," the Lora Locke management simply busted out a wall between two single rooms.

"We still call it the Willard Scott Suite," said the woman with the beehive. "It has a view of the stockyards south of town. We charged him double, of course." Of course. With the Lora Locke closed, Fred and I headed out of Dodge for the circa-1886 Cimarron Hotel & Restaurant in Cimarron, just 18 miles west of Dodge—not far, by the way, from the Holcomb, Kansas of Truman Capote's *In Cold Blood*. The Cimarron Hotel is now a bed-and-breakfast run by one Kathi Holt. We rented a room for $35. The next day was Sunday and so we got the pleasure of taking the huge dinner the Cimarron Hotel serves for the grand price of $7. Somebody had had the presence of mind to call ahead and ask Holt to put fresh calf fries (bull-calf testicles, also known as prairie oysters) on the menu.

"We got them right out of the pasture yesterday," said Holt. "Is that fresh enough?" Seemed so to us. The next day we would go north toward Nebraska.

PAXTON, NEBRASKA

"Does the elk have a name?" I asked the waitress. Fred and I were sitting beneath one of 100 or so stuffed animal heads that jut out from the walls of Ole's Big Game Lounge in western Nebraska just off Interstate 80. We had found our way to Paxton via Ogallala, which—like Dodge City—is an old 19th-century cattle town complete with a Boot Hill and a halfhearted tourist look about it.

Ole's must be one of the few politically incorrect public places left in America. Small children wander in and out among adults throwing back anything but white wine. Behind the bar are girlie-calendar pictures. Marlboro country means the cloud of cigarette smoke could by itself cause global warming. The animal heads mounted on the walls throughout the restaurant are from all over the world, each personally shot by the lounge's owner, one Ole Herstedt. It is the kind of place that would drive both Jane Fonda and Dan Quale nuts.

"Not the elk," said the waitress. "The kids named the buffalo 'Bill,' but nobody's named the elk."

"He's about to name it," said Fred. "He names everything. My truck is called Squirrel Tooth."

"I see," said the waitress.

"I name the elk 'Fred,'" I said.

"See?" said Fred.

"'Fred' it is," the waitress said. "You guys ready for a drink?"

We were. Red ones. Tomato beers: two-thirds beer to one-third tomato juice.

It is the drink of choice on the High Plains. The waitress nodded and left for the bar. Fred pulled out his WPA guides to Kansas and Nebraska. He was going to study where we had been and where we were going. It was a long day to get to Paxton and Ole's (and the Gingerbread Inn next to the railroad tracks, where we would stay and the next morning have pancakes the size of a full moon). We had made a 300-mile swing, starting off in Woodston, Kan., and, in an itinerary suggested by the Kansas WPA Guide, taking U.S. 36 west. First stop, a few miles north of the highway, was Herndon, where we took lunch at the Pool Hall tavern. Then we were off to Bone Hill ("so named for a pile of buffalo bones at its base. According to tradition, these are the bones of an entire herd of buffalo stampeded over the bluff by Indian hunters").

From Bone Hill, we went on through Bird City ("the former home of Banty Rogers...the man who taught Charles A. Lindbergh aeronautics. After his transAtlantic flight, Lindbergh flew over Bird City in ...the *Spirit of St. Louis,* and dropped a note of tribute to his old teacher"), and then into St. Francis. Out of St. Francis, a heat-baked town in the far northwestern corner of Kansas, we took a 90-degree turn north along Route 27 past a home-made historical marker on the site of the last buffalo killed in Kansas, and then through the Breaks, as the low hills along the Arikaree River are locally called, into Nebraska. There, east of Haigler, at the historical marker at Texas Canyon, we found a spiral notebook kept in a wooden box so that visitors can comment on the history that was made by the cowboys along the Ogallala cattle trail 100 years before. One entry I copied out read: 6/19/92 *Ron and Elsa Bennett. Visited here and camped overnight. Homeless we are and unemployed as well as stranger to be the rest of my life without choice, unless jobs or the work in this country improves.*

The waitress brought our beers. "Where are we?" I said when I saw that Fred had pulled out one of his maps.

"Not all that far from Senator George W. Norris's home in McCook," he said. "McCook also had the first Frank Lloyd Wright house built west of the Mississippi."

"Do they go together?" I said.

"Both progressives on behalf of the people," said Fred. He was about to tell me about Norris, a five-term U.S. senator who spanned the WPA era, and how the Plains states could produce such admirable people (even if they were Republicans), but I was out to tease him.

"Didn't Nebraska have a senator," I asked, "who argued that a mediocre Supreme Court judge should be appointed to represent the views of mediocre citizens?" Fred's eyes narrowed.

"Roman Hruska," said Fred. "It was over the Carswell nomination. We won't talk about it."

He folded up his maps. The difference between us on politics (as I've heard Fred say himself) is that Fred can't enjoy the dark irony that Hruska's views finally prevailed in the bloom of George Bush's Supreme Court appointments. I decided not to push it. Fred laid into his red beer. The waitress took our orders: calf fries again, this time with steaks. Infidelity for a couple of paunchy, middle-aged married men had been reduced to cheating on the American Heart Association's diet.

The next day we did indeed spend most of a pleasant afternoon in the late Senator Norris's home and in the delightful Museum of the High Plains—so true to homestead frugality that you turn on the lights section by section as you walk through, turning them off as you leave. On our way out of McCook, we drove by the Frank Lloyd Wright house: Its beauty is stunning, yet not in the least out of place in this otherwise two-story-frame-house town. I think Senator Norris would have approved. He probably did.

THE RETURN OF FRED: GOVE, KANSAS

"How are the time rocks?" I say. Fred has pulled Squirrel Tooth
up in front of my theater seat and is leaning out the window. The
shadows from the buildings have grown fat in the setting sun so
that all of the town—what there is left of it—is filled with them.

"What?" he says.

"The time rocks," I say. "At the Santa Fe station."

"I forgot about them," he says. "Did I ever tell you about
Mysterious Dave Mather and the Sunday he. . ."

I get up from my seat and stretch my legs. About an hour before,
a fickle wind finally blew the store's We Are Closed note my way
and I nabbed it: "Gone to Kansas City for Royals game. Be open
Monday. Vote Perot." I think about handing it over to Fred, but
I decide I'll save it for the drive home—something to start talk
between Fort Hays and Junction City; the history of baseball in
America, Kansas City and "Mr. and Mrs. Bridge," the politics of
Harry Truman. Maybe we'll talk about what we keep looking for
out here. Probably not. Next trip.

"Have a good time?" I say as I get in of my side of the truck.

"I did," he says. "You?'

"As well," I say. Ahead against the window of the truck, I see the
movie of where we have been and wish I could stay there forever.

Carrie Nation

Today her notoriety and fame rest largely on the cartoon image she forged in the nation's press in the early 1900s: a long brass-rail bar lies wasted; broken glasses and bottles and split kegs festoon the floor; the bartender peeks up in front of a shattered mirror; a painting of a nude seems to have a hatchet cleft in it; worried patrons gather outside at the busted-out front window to see what's what; and in the middle of all this stands a huge-headed woman with a hatchet in her right hand and what appear to be pool-table stanchions for legs under a plain black skirt. The caption reads: "I cannot tell a lie-I did it with my little hatchet!"

In western Kansas not far from Kiowa, where in the early 20th century Carry A. Nation first wielded her hatchet in the service of saloon smashing, a local business has displayed a sign that reads: DAMM—Drunks Against Mad Mothers. Mrs. Nation would not be amused, although she might grudgingly admire the defiant stance the perpetrators profess. Carry Nation was defiance personified.

Known at the start of her career mainly as a leader of the women's temperance movement, Carry became an international figure. Her exploits in demolishing "joints," giving lectures, selling hatchets, publishing a weekly newspaper *(The Smashers Mail)*, being horsewhipped and getting tossed into jails all over the

United States made her one of the most celebrated and talked-about women of her time.

Lost in the publicity of that time—and even today—are the notable and abiding ethical tenets that Carry Nation espoused. Among them: women don't have to endure beatings by drunken husbands; women don't have to see the wages meant for their families spent in taverns; men don't have to form clubs and cliques based on sex and race, and then confirm the authority of such clubs by toasts and revelry; the homeless need a place to live; the young need sex education; alcoholism is a disease; smoking is bad for you; women have equal rights.

Like all extremists, Carry Nation was right to the point of being wrong. Some feminists think that between Prohibition and Carry's strident politics, women's rights got set back 50 years. Maybe. But in her time Carry Nation indelibly laid upon the American conscience some nagging and largely unresolved questions about the use of drugs, the roles of men and women in marriage, not to mention the viability of direct political action. Carry was our century's first moral crusader; measured against her sense of "commitment," our latter day moralists—majority or otherwise—are thin malt by comparison.

Born Carry Amelia Moore in Garrard County, Kentucky, on November 25, 1846, Carry was reared by a father who was first a planter and later an itinerant livestock trader, and a mother who frequently took herself to be Queen Victoria. The family decided the best course in regard to Carry's mother was to make the same assumption she did: slaves were occasionally dressed up as palace guards, the Queen's rooms were furnished with something like the trappings of royalty. Audiences were held, local farmers knighted and Prince Albert (Carry's father, George Moore, in his other life) consulted about the fate of the natives in such far-flung empires as Missouri and Texas.

There were other incidents of family oddity: an aunt got to thinking she was a weather vane; a male cousin decided in his 40s that the best method of locomotion was to return to all fours. He was finally talked out of it by a minister who held his tête-a-têtes at ground level; and by Carry herself, who more or less lived with the family's black servants until she was 7, and was a special friend of Uncle Josh—a slightly mad, elderly black man who seemed to come and go in the house as he pleased. On the whole, life among the Moores was not the sane and stable influence that one hopes for in a future reformer—though it perhaps gave Carry some of the dramatic flair she later put to the service of her causes. It may also have given her license for the self-delusion that largely deprived her of serious consideration by the public, even that part of the public that was sympathetic to her most humane causes.

Although it is true that in some respects Carry Nation is the grandmother of our recent concern about the excessive use of drugs in general—and of alcohol in particular (as exemplified by the flourishing chapters of Mothers against Drunk Driving)—it seems clear in retrospect that her first and continuing impulse was to befriend the woebegone and homeless.

In Medicine Lodge, Kansas, where she and her second husband, David Nation, settled in the 1890s, she was known as "Mother Nation" —not a name of irony or derision, but one that celebrated her generosity. In Kansas, as in the years before in Missouri and Texas, Carry's instincts were to look out after the poor and battered, especially women. Medicine Lodge saw her establish a sewing circle to make clothes for the destitute. Her strong belief in education (she was once a teacher) led her to make it her business that few children in Medicine Lodge had to stay home from school for want of proper clothing. At Thanksgiving and Christmas the downtrodden were invited into the Nation home for a generous feast. David Nation was at this time one of the town's preachers, and such hospitality was no doubt part of his calling. But even then Carry was more than just a preacher's wife. She had already developed a belief that the disadvantaged need practical care. And a voice.

"I represent the distracted, suffering, loving motherhood of the World," Carry Nation wrote in her autobiography, *The Use and Need of the Life of Carry A. Nation,* which, though she revised it seven times, remains (along with Robert Lewis Taylor's *Vessel of Wrath*) one of the best accounts of Carry's life and times.

Her autobiography, as well as independent documents, depict a woman marched through the last third of her life with a dichotomous character forged in childhood. In her early years, she was sickly; as an adult she was an ox of physical strength. As a school girl she was sometimes speechless, as a mature woman she was wicked with words. When a young lady, she became the sycophantic bride of a drunk; in old age, she ripped the cigars out of men's mouths.

Carry spent a year in bed during girlhood nursing an unspecified illnesss labeled "consumption of the bowels" by a local doctor. Among the cures proposed was a kind of exorcism in which indigenous religious personages argued that unless Carry repented her youthful penchant for thievery around the Moore home her illness would last a lifetime. She repented with gusto; so much so that in later years if she found an item around the house that was not hers and whose owner she could not locate, she'd give it away rather than keep it. But if the remedy later took, it was not at the time, and Carry stayed groaning in bed.

Next, the adults tried to cure Carry with a winter baptism in an iced creek. The ordeal gave her a start on the visions she was to experience throughout her life, but soon she was back in bed for much of the next three years. Nothing seemed to work but time: on one of her family's frequent moves, in this case from Texas to

Missouri, poor Carry at age 15 seemed to simply grow out of her malady.

As a mature woman Carry Nation was anything but sickly. She was tall and hefty, as strong as she was homely. Her physical prowess in tearing up saloons made splendid copy from coast to coast. On one occassion she picked up a heavy iron cash register and tossed it into the street. She was good at flinging billard balls, brickbats and hatchets. A bartender who planned to shoot her during one of her raids panicked and fired his pistol into the ceiling when he saw her rip the door off an ice chest. The bedridden days of her youth were redeemed with a vengeance in the prime of her life.

As a schoolgirl, Carry was once left shamed and speechless by the request of a teacher that she present one side of a debating topic (something to do with whether dogs and cats had reasoning faculties and therefore could go to Heaven). Carry was supposed to argue that they did and could. "When I was called," she wrote in her autobiography, "I know I looked ridiculously blank...All [my classmates] burst out in uncontrollable laughter. I went to my seat, put my face in my arms and turned my back to the audience. I wept tears of humiliation. I felt disgraced. I thought of what a shame this would be to my parents...These things nerved me. I dried my tears, turned around in my seat, looked up, and the moral force it required to do this was almost equal to that which smashed a saloon." Pets found their way to Heaven.

Her resolve to be always prepared to make her case lasted into later life. At the height of her career, Carry Nation was an extraordinary speaker, able to hold throngs spellbound by both her message and her delivery. On behalf of the temperance movement, she toured not only the United States but England and Scotland as well. At worst, she was something of a sideshow (she once lectured at Coney Island). At best, she could swap insults like pistol fire and ambush the unlucky. Among the unfortunates were Mrs. Alfred Vanderbilt and other women in her party at a Madison Square Garden horse show in the fall of 1902. The issue was extravagant dress; no doubt the Vanderbilts were fashion plates for the event. But after a lifetime of raising money to clothe the poor and of helping to house the homeless, and with more than a modicum of moral indignation over what Carry thought was wrongheaded behavior and just plain "setting a bad example," she lit into the hapless social and financial lions as they sat peacefully in their reserved box hoping to watch the horses prance.

"You think you are well dressed," said Carry, standing before the startled women, "but you ought to be ashamed of yourselves for wearing such disgraceful clothes. Take them off at once and dress yourselves more modestly."

The tirade didn't stop there. Carry, at the time a figure whose glowering physiognomy was recognized on the streets of New York by public and press alike, began wandering around Madison Square Garden searching for more affronts to her sensibility. As she did so, she gathered an entourage of bemused onlookers as well as the New York press. Like their Kansas counterparts, the New York reporters regularly spelled her name "Carrie," and they would gleefully steer her to the nearest saloon in order to write a first-hand account of the carnage that was sure to follow. As she toured, Carry delivered a running monologue about the various evils: drink, excessive dress, the devil in general. This from a woman who had once burst into tears when asked to recite in class.

Perhaps the most significant instance in which Carry's crusading character was formed by her early life was her first marriage. At age 19 she fell in love with one Dr. Charles Gloyd, a sot who managed to hide the full flower of his condition until after they were married. Gloyd was a boarder at the Moore home in Missouri. His idea was to take a position in a nearby school until he could decide where in the area he might like to set up medical practice. All this seemed reasonable enough—except to Carry's mother, Queen Victoria. In a moment of clarity she spotted Dr. Gloyd for what he was and issued a Royal proclamation that the two should never be alone together. It worked, sort of.

One day during the two-year courtship, Gloyd caught his future bride in the house and gave her a kiss. Carry screamed, "I am ruined! I am ruined!" As was her lifelong penchant, she had overstated the case. In fact, she apparently rather liked the physical attention. From then on (the Royal ban was still in effect) the two conducted their affair by leaving notes for each other in the Moores' copy of Shakespeare. They dropped hints as to where the messages could be found by comments at the dinner table on what passages they had been lately reading, and in the end were married—apparently without the Queen's blessing.

Gloyd was drunk at his wedding. Carry notes that when they were married "... his countenance was not bright, he was changed." Further, she describes her wedding day as "one of the gloomiest I ever saw." And, not surprisingly, Gloyd disappointed her in bed. She writes that her longing for the physical attention of Gloyd made her "hungry for his caresses." In later years she claimed to have found many other women in much the same state, and even argued that women who strayed into prostitution did so because of the neglect of drunken husbands.

Her views on the matter of sex were surprisingly liberal. She was an advocate of sex education—not only for newlyweds, but for children as well. Tales of babies being found in hollow trees or being brought by storks were anathema to Carry: "Talk freely," she advised parents concerning the instruction of children about sex. "Truth will purify everything it comes in contact with. Ignorance is not innocence, but is the promoter of crime." And here—as she often did throughout her life, she quoted the Bible: "'My people are destroyed for lack of knowledge.' Hosea 4:6."

Gloyd became more and more of a drunk. He wouldn't come

home except to sleep off his binges. He hid from his patients, taking refuge from his wife and most everybody else by repairing to the local Masonic Lodge. Carry would troop down there and try to get any men she found heading inside to drag Gloyd out—but without much luck. She left him when their baby was 6 weeks old and returned to live with her parents. "Pet," said Gloyd in begging for yet another chance, "if you leave me, I will be a dead man in six months." He was more or less accurate in his prediction. But Carry's mother had somehow had the good sense to counsel her not to return to the pleading doctor. Carry raised the child, a girl—mentally and physically debilitated, as fate would have it—with her second husband.

It is for her opposition to alcoholic beverages, of course, that Carry Nation is best known. However, to suggest that she brooded over her early rotten marriage to a drunken husband and took it out on the rest of American manhood is to misjudge her best impulses. Even with Gloyd and their sick child, Carry's attitude was medically modern: "Oh," she exclaimed, "the curse that comes through heredity, and this liquor evil, a disease that entails more depravity on children unborn, than all else, unless it be tobacco." Elsewhere she wrote: "I did not know then that drinking men were drugged men, diseased men."

Her second husband, David Nation, was a lawyer, a journalist, a farmer and a preacher—-and not very good at anything. They moved to Columbia, Texas, where Carry took in boarders and fed the drifters. Later, in Richmond, Texas, she ran a hotel, cooked and cleaned and nursed, and saw the raw edges of male life on the Western frontier. It made her sick—and angry—deepening her social consciousness. By the time the Nations picked up their belongings and headed for Kansas in 1893, Carry was Robert Lewis Taylor's "vessel of wrath" about to explode. In Medicine Lodge where they settled, poor David would try to preach his sermons, but Carry wouldn't let him. Sitting in the congregation she'd correct and amplify what he had to say. If David objected, Carry would announce the service was over and sometimes, it was reported, marched her husband out the door. Clearly, she had had enough of male superiority and was hovering on the lunatic fringe. But just as clearly, her most important work lay ahead of her.

Officially, Kansas was a dry state. You couldn't buy intoxicants over the counter except for medicinal purposes, like for rabies or typhoid or, say, a case of the blues from drinking too much the night before. The laws were a joke and nobody bothered to enforce them. In Medicine Lodge—as in most of Kansas—there were "joints" that sold liquor. This, after all, was Kansas—then still very much part of the West (Hays, not too far from where Carry lived, had been known as the Sodom of the plains).

What Carry tried to do—first with the assistance of the other women in town and later more or less on her own—was to get the Kansas laws enforced. If you discount the violence of her tongue, her early efforts were peaceful. She took a beating in terms of popular ridicule, and often a physical one as well. Her efforts produced a mixed result and to large parts of the public she was a laughingstock.

But on June 6, 1899, Carry Nation awoke to a "musical" voice, one that "seemed to be speaking in [her] heart." It told her to go south 20-odd miles to Kiowa, Kansas—a perpetually sleepy town near the Oklahoma border. To Carry, the voice was God telling her what to do next in her fight against the Kansas joints. In addition to His commandment to go to Kiowa, God added the following assurance: "I'll stand by you." Carry concluded—with more than a little poetic license—that all together God's remarks could be interpreted to mean: "Take something in your hands, and throw [it] at these places in Kiowa and smash them."

Carry spent the rest of the morning wrapping brickbats in newspapers. That afternoon, with a horse and buggy, she made the trip to Kiowa. On her way she had visions of demons gathered along the road. Later, she asked for another sign from God, a sort of confirmation that she had heard Him right the first time and that Kiowa was the town whose bars were to be righteously smashed. If God wanted her to continue, then her horse was to pass unguided (at least by Carry) through a particular gate on the road. He did and they both arrived at Kiowa later that night.

The next morning (June 7) Carry went into a saloon operated by one Mr. Dobson. She laid out her balls of rock-bearing paper (she called them "smashers") and delivered to a startled Mr. Dobson a lecture on the evils of drink. When she concluded, she rifled the smashers at the bottles and glasses and mirrors of Mr. Dobson's saloon. The result was liquid carnage—and a draught of history.

But broken glass and running whiskey and a terrified Dobson were not what Carry saw as she trashed her first joint. Instead: "I saw Mr. McKinley, the President, sitting in an old-fashioned arm chair and as the stones would strike I saw them hit the chair and the chair fell to pieces, and I saw Mr. McKinley fall over." As ready with interpretation as she was with vision, Carry tells us what it all meant: ". . . smashing in Kansas was intended to strike the head of this nation the hardest blow, for every saloon I smashed in Kansas had a license from the head of this government ..."

Thus armed, Carry Nation began her assault on the country at large.

These days Kansas is "wet"—or partially so. Kiowa itself is a peaceful small town with a large rock commemorating Carry's adventures. Near the site of Dobson's saloon is the Uptown Recreation Club (the euphemism perhaps a legacy of Carry's wrath). It is a local bar, full of pool tables and girlie posters, that pushes beer. Patrons of the Uptown drink the local concoction: tomato juice and beer. Red Ones, they are called.

In Kiowa, as in the rest of the country, no doubt there are men drinking up their weekly checks instead of paying off the note at the bank. No doubt there are lonely and discouraged wives out on the Kansas farms trying to raise a family with the burden of an alcoholic husband. Carry's battle seems lost—at least in the territory where she first fought for the cause that made her famous. But perhaps not entirely. Although we have usually regarded Carry Nation as little more than an uncommon scold about drinking and smoking, her highly visible rage may have pointed the way for a more mature national debate on these matters.

"I believe I have always failed in everything I undertook to do the first time," Carry wrote, "but I learned only by experience, paid dearly for it and valued it afterwards."

It would be reassuring if we could believe those are the words of a woman who grew wise with age. But it is hard to forget the outrageousness of her later years. Once, on a visit to New York City, Carry threatened random "hatchetation" unless the Hotel Victoria (irony always had a way of cropping up around our heroine) clothed the naked statue of Diana that adorned its lobby. Not wanting to join the Dobson saloons of the world, the Victoria did so with tantalizing folds of cheesecloth. Flushed with victory, Carry held a press conference at which she sang the following:

Sing a song of six joints,
With bottles full of rye;
Four and twenty beer kegs,
Stacked up on the sly.
When the kegs were opened,
The beer began to sing,
Hurrah for Carry Nation,
Her work beats anything.

"Gertrude"

Author's Note:
The Last Cattle Drive

In 1977 Putnam, Inc. in New York published my novel *The Last Cattle Drive.* It was not (and is not) a best seller as some blurbs had said, but it was a good enough book to go though many editions and to stay in print over thirty years. I wrote "*The Last Cattle Drive* Stampede" for *KS Magazine*; it is about the first time *The Last Cattle Drive* was not made into a movie. By now the number of subsequent times it has not been made into a movie is more or less equal to the number of editions of the novel— maybe, for all I know, the number of years the novel has been in print. Even as I am typing these words there is another director trying to work out the details for the movie. The book is now famous in Hollywood as the most filmable novel not made into a movie even written.

I wrote the "Route of *The Last Cattle Drive*" for the publication of the special 30th anniversary edition of the novel. My thanks to Fred Woodward at the University Press of Kansas for suggesting the project, and for keeping the novel in print these last years.

The Last Cattle Drive Stampede

I forget how I first heard that my novel *The Last Cattle Drive* (an account of a modern day cattle drive from Western Kansas to Kansas City complete with accounts of famous Kansas Thump-Thump contests) was being considered as a film project, but I remember hearing that Xerox copies of the typescript were being sent to the West Coast by plane. Not airmail. And not Federal Express because this was in the late '70s and before all that.

My impression was that some Great Film Company had booked a seat for a stack of typescripts on the evening flight from New York to L.A. First class, no doubt. There was, I heard, to be an auction. Unless someone—A Great Movie Someone I was led to believe (and at one time I even knew his name)—unless A Great Movie Someone decided instead to go to the south of France to play boules. Weeks went by and nothing happened. All was quiet on the rumor front. My book went through the normal publication processes. Apparently boules was being played in the South of France. Or maybe there had been an auction and nobody wanted to buy my particular kind of bull. I was told the novel would now go around the lot. In any case, not to worry. My book had "rooting interest."

In retrospect I recognize a basic absurdity that should have foretold for me the future: I never thought that The Great Movie

People were in fact reading my novel—in Xeroxed first class typescript or in its final published form. What I thought was that the Great Movie Someone needed a stack of pages to wave at a Great Movie Someone Else and talk a lot in movie mumble about taking meetings on this coast or that coast baby until finally A Not So Great Movie Someone got a Monarch Notes report from someone who had in fact read the book (that someone is so far down the end of the reel that he doesn't even get an adjective— and besides "he" is probably a "she"). In the end lots of typescript waving goes on until, say, George C. Scott says yes. Or no. He said no. But not before he said maybe. But that comes later.

Two confessions: one, all this was in the days shortly after *Annie Hall* came out and so my picture of the movie business is shot through Woody Allen's camera, and two, there are a few good guys in all this: my agent, for one. He told me in the beginning many are called and none are chosen and Hollywood is all madness. Go back to your typewriter, he would say. Of course. Easily done when your novel is being considered for a movie. Right. My agent lives in New York; he's not sure Los Angeles exists but if it does he doesn't approve.

"I just had a talk with the movie people," I said to him one day.

"Yes," he said.

"They didn't seem to know how matters stood. I got angry," I said.

"Yes," he said.

"I might have been rude," I said.

"They wouldn't know," he said. "They have no culture and no conversation."

The other good guy is a good lady: an independent producer who did in fact read the book, bought it for her Great Film Company and as far as I know to this day thinks the novel would make a fine movie. Along the way she had a heart attack and 10 to the power 20 anxiety attacks. Her story is no doubt more maddening than mine. But first in print as we say in the writing business.

Sometime after The *Last Cattle Drive* was published and long after the Great Movie Someone had come back from his boules, I was standing in a friend's car repair garage when his phone rang. It was for me. The switch board operator at Washington College in Maryland where I teach had tracked me down to say that Hollywood was on another line and did I want to speak to them. She hoped I did because by now they had invested a few dollars on the wait. Put them on I said. Hollywood calling, I told my friend who was refurbishing a splendid old Morgan.

A woman agent I didn't know wanted me to hear the news hot: The *Last Round Up* had been sold. For X dollars with various options. It was a great day. She had been told it was a great book. It would make a fine movie. It had rooting interest. On behalf of her agency (who was aligned with my agent) she wanted to thank me. I was impressed. Even if she'd gotten the title wrong. I'd never had X dollars before and although I understood that only a tiny millimeter of the X's leg was to come my way at the beginning, still I thought that when the whole X gets in my pocket I'll be a rich man. And that, I knew, was only the beginning. Your mind does funny things at a moment like this. I'd al*ways* wanted an airplane. I saw myself at the controls of a Lear Jet going toward Cannes.

A day later the woman agent called back to say that she had boosted the price to a slightly bigger X. It was a great day. The more Xs loaded on the film the better. Still, all these Xs, much like the verbs in a German sentence, came at the end. A few days later the lady producer called to say she had been the one who had bought the book and how pleased she was at having done so. It had been sent to her by an urban cowboy from Texas who thought it wonderful in spite of its slanderous attitude towards Texans. She'd let me know when there was more news.

A few days later my agent called to tell me that all the film people who had been calling me the previous week were for once in their lives correct about something: the book had been optioned. Not sold, he pointed out. Optioned. They were renting it with an option to buy. It might take years for them to make up their minds, and just because they got something right this time don't count on it next time. Go back to your typewriter, he advised, and forget about it. Right. Just forget that your book is going to be made into a movie and that one day you'll be sitting in the theater watching Robert Mitchum, Cloris Leachman, Jimmy Stewart, and Timothy Hutton (my ideal cast in those days) parading across the screen on your words. That vision and the vision of all those Xs just dropped out of my mind. Right.

Months went by. I called The Great Film Company. It was a good thing, too. George C. Scott was 90-percent a sure thing to play the lead. With him in the picture all else would fall in place. It would be the Patton of Westerns. Richard Nixon would watch it. If I had not called I might have begun a slow drift toward my typewriter. Four days later came the only letter over a period of five years that I was to get from Hollywood. George C. Scott had advised The Great Film Company he was not going to do the picture. It was a matter of creative control—whatever that was. Off the screen went my vision of Scott doing a parody of the scene toward the end of *Patton* where he gives an interview on a horse. Or hearing him say as he drives the steers through the streets of Kansas City: "I love it, God help me, I love it." George, how could you? Poor Richard Nixon. (If he finds out he'll have a seventh crisis.)

Several more months go by. I get a message to call a number in New York. I am to ask for a Mr. Skins. It is about the movie.

"Al's," says a voice. There is music in the background and loud talk.

"Mr. Skins, please," I say.

"You want Skins?" the man says.

"I'm returning his call," I say.

"He's in the head," I can hear someone in the room say. I take it I have reached a pay phone. The man who has answered has apparently let the phone drop to the end of its cord. It swings back and forth and I hear it thud when it hits a wall.

"Hello, Skins here," says a man who turns out not to be Mr. Skins but just Skins.

"Robert Day returning your call," I say.

"Yes," he says. "Glad you called. I've got a partner and we've got a little showcase picture business whereby we use a dynamite story like your *Last Round Up* book and plop one of our actors in the middle and take it the film festival route. Cannes. Venice. South Florida."

"It's called *The Last Cattle Drive*," I say.

"Fine. Good. B plus title. We might have to nix that. Westerns aren't in right now. But what do you say you come up to New York and we treat you to a little meal and talk the matter over."

"I have an agent," I say. "You should call him."

"I can't do agents," says Skins. "I think its best we work this ourselves. Agents get in the way. We can spring for your bus ticket here. You in Kansas, right."

"Maryland," I say.

"Really. Drive up then. We'll pay gas, tolls, the works."

"Can't do it," I say. I was about to tell him the book had already been bought, but there was some commotion in the bar and he said he had to go. He'd call back. It will take awhile but he will.

More months go by. By now the rent on the book is up and The Great Film Company either has to pay X or let it go. Or, as it turns out by the contract, they can rent it again for another year while they get their act together. They do the latter. About the same time I get another phone call—this time from the lady producer. Good news. They've hired a screen play writer. I didn't know they wanted a screenplay writer. I thought they were looking for cattle and actors. If they wanted a screenplay writer why didn't they call me? I could have done that. But they have hired Robert Getchell: *Bound For Glory. Alice Doesn't Live Here Anymore.* He grew up in Missouri. Missouri, I say. My book is about Kansas. Not to worry he knows about Kansas. We are lucky to get him. He cost us a pound of flesh and two pounds of Xs. The more Xs we load on the picture the more likely it is to get made. John Travolta is interested. I call my agent.

"Who is John Travolta?" he says. You have to know my agent. He likes books above all. It would ruin his day to know about John Travolta. Never mind, I say. Go back to your typewriter he says.

Six months later I get a call. They have a script. They are pleased with it. I will be pleased with it. It has some of my own words therein. I will recognize my story. Paul Newman is interested. Burt Reynolds is interested. They've changed the name of the project. *Last Cattle Drive* sounds too much like a Western. It's called *Road Show*. They'll send me a script.

True, the script does have some of my words and true as well I recognize the story. Some of the characters, however, are a bit more difficult to find: my 40-year-old Cloris Leachman is now a 25-year-old Jessica Lange and my old cowboy's prostrate cancer becomes the nameless dread (Jimmy Stewart groans and bends over out of the frame now and then, but nobody says anything). But the thing that really irks me is that Kansas Thump-Thump (you have to read the book to understand the rules) is changed to Missouri Mule. Who ever heard of Missouri Mule? Everybody knows about Kansas Thump-Thump. Six more months go by. I get a call.

John Travolta is no longer interested but we didn't want him anyway. He's going to do another western: something about a city cowboy. Paul Newman thinks the project will be too easy. Cher is a picture away from a major role and she's ready to take Cloris Leachman's part if Faye Dunaway doesn't want it. Sally Field has turned down the female lead but accepted the male lead. The picture is on the board to be made in Kansas in September or Texas in November depending on how things break. It's a GO project for The Great Film Company. About this time *Heaven's Gate* opens in New York. The silence for the next year is going to be astounding. No western will be made anywhere, no matter what month, no matter how things break, no matter how GREAT the film company or how GO the project.

"They want to renew the option," says my agent late that summer.

"What about my Xs," I say.

"It's bad for writers to think about Xs," says my agent.

"Are they going to make the picture this fall?" I say.

"Nobody's going to make a western ever again," says my agent.

"*Heaven's Gate?*" I say.

"It used up all the western's money until the turn of the century," says my agent.

"Why? Do they want to extend the option?" I say.

"Madness," he says.

The picture was not made in Kansas that fall. Or in Texas. *Heaven's Gate* was a Black Hole for Xs, down which my movie fell and out of which came no sound from anyone in Hollywood.

One winter night Skins calls back.

"We're still interested," he says.

"Talk to my agent," I say.

"We still don't talk to agents," he says.

"A Great Film Company has bought the picture," I say. "They're making the movie."

"We could do a showcase half-hour with Teddy Grumpelt. You heard of Teddy Grumpelt?'

"No," I say. There is some noise in the bar and shouting. I think Skins wants more change for the phone. On credit no doubt. Then I hear the clink of coins.

"You come to New York," he says. "We'll spring for a dinner at Chez Poulet. You heard of Chez Poulet?"

"No," I say.

"It's a steak place," he says. "It's got good Kansas City steak. That's what a good Kansas boy needs. Kansas beef. Don't take your book to Hollywood, kid. They'll break your heart." In the background there is more noise. I suppose his credit runs out. The phone lines turn to a buzz.

More months go by. Another option is renewed. Then the option is picked up. By now 18 percent inflation and four years have raised hell with my X. One whole leg is missing.

But not to worry: the big basket of Xs is to be gathered when the picture is made. Paperback editions in seven languages. T-shirts and cowboy dolls. My Lear Jet takes off in many directions. Meanwhile the Great Film Company fires the lady producer. She leaves with the picture as part of her golden parachute. She starts all over, this time on her own. She calls to tell me that Marty Ritt is interested in directing the movie. That is good news. If Ritt takes the project it will get made. There is no mention of actors which, I am beginning to think, is the real good news.

However, in the meantime, not only have I been getting calls from a bar in New York, but I've been getting them from Ireland as well. The connections are never good and the brogue is thick so I'm not entirely sure what gets said, but the gist of it is that the caller, an Irish producer, knows an English director who in turn knows some French actors who once played boules with a Great American Movie Some One in the south of France and between games they discussed the possibility of making a modern western in northern Italy. I can't puzzle out if the cowboys will be bossing my herd in Italian, French or the Queen's English, but somehow I get the impression they are going to make their movie version of my book no matter what Hollywood does. This I know is wrong, a violation of international rights that will keep plagues of California movie lawyers busy for generations. I know as well I should tell my Hollywood producer, my agent, maybe even Rona Barrett. But I say nothing. Your mind does funny things at moments like these: I see myself smiling as my cattle drive roars through the Chianti wine district toward Siena. "Prego, prego," says a tall Italian cowboy.

It is about this time Jack Nicholson enters the picture. He and Marty Ritt have lunch in the Russian Tea Room and a deal is cut. A Very Great Film Company will bank it. Timothy Hutton is on board. They are looking to rope in a rising star of a woman. Cher's name comes up again. *Variety* says she's taken the part. *Variety* says she's not taken the part. The picture is set for Kansas in May. I get lots of calls. One day driving along in a friend's restored Morgan I hear on the local radio news more than you'd ever want to know about the making of my picture. A week later in an airplane the hostess hands me a copy of *USA Today* where I find the movie is a front page story: Nicholson and Hutton are in Kansas. There is a map of the state in case the rest of the nation doesn't know where it is. Nicholson buys sweatshirts at the University of Kansas bookstore and flirts with the cashier. Hutton takes pictures of the prairie so he can have them blown up and hung on the walls of his Malibu beach house. He wants to get the feel of Kansas, he says. The Very Great Film Company gets Topeka, Kansas to pass a law allowing cattle to be driven through its streets. The Very Great Film Company buys a herd. It is a GO project My basket of Xs is getting full.

"Any difference between steers and cattle?" says a man's voice at the other end of the phone. "This is pre-production calling."

"Yes," I say. "The words are different, that should tell you something."

"We bought cattle and someone says *your* book says steers. Have we got trouble?"

"Do the cattle you bought have large bags hanging between their back legs?" I say.

"I don't know," he says. "I'm in California."

"Call your man in Kansas and ask about the bags. No bags, no trouble. Unless you got sold 250 bulls, which I doubt."

"You are our man in Kansas," he says.

"I'm in Maryland," I say.

"What a mess," he says.

Again, months go by. More newspaper and television stories. The movie gets put back until late summer. They want the feel of heat in the footage. Marty Ritt quits. Health reasons. Who can blame him. He probably had a clause that said any place but Kansas in late summer. Not to worry. Nicholson is driving the picture. It is going to go. The *Very* Great Film Company office in New York calls to thank me for writing such a filmable book. It has rooting interest. Some day he hopes to read it.

In mid-summer they hire another director. I forget his name. Nobody important. He looks over the script and says it's sick. Then he gets sick.

Or so *Variety* says. He says he's not sick. It's the script that's sick. But no matter, the cattle are ready to go, the streets of Topeka have been cleared. Movie production is to begin on Monday, August 25th, 1982.

It is Sunday, August 24th. The phone rings. It is difficult for me to write this. Hello, I say. It is a pal in Kansas.

"They are selling the cattle."

"What cattle?" I say.

"The picture's cattle."

"Why?" I say. Boy, am I dumb.

"The radio says it's because they're not going to make the movie after all."

Your mind does funny things at moments like this. There are no words in my head. Instead, I see an Italian cowboy riding up to a New York café—Chez Poulet. He throws a boule through the window. Great Movie People dressed as steers rush out into the street. Crowds of bystanders root them on. My agent is there, trying to pull me out of the way. To no avail. I rope a steer as a souvenir of what might have been. When caught it is lighter than air and floats upward taking me with it.

"What movie?" I say.

The Route of *The Last Cattle Drive*

One autumn day in the early 1980s I took my pickup truck along the route of *The Last Cattle Drive*. I wanted to see what mistakes I had made in the details I had used in the novel. And what fiction I had mapped for the drive to follow. Was the schoolyard in Paradise, Kansas, the way I recorded it? More or less. Was there a boardinghouse down the road should the characters want a place to stay that first night? No. Was it possible to have a motor home run into the herd near Lake Wilson? Yes. Was it probable there were pheasants near Blackwolf?

"We don't get many pheasant hunters around here," said a rancher I met at a coffee shop in Wilson. "Better shooting north and west. Try Hays."

Later that day I drove into Brookville and, like the characters in the novel, had a chicken dinner at the celebrated Brookville Hotel albeit without Opal, Jed, and Spangler. Or Sissy. Just as I was paying my bill someone from the restaurant asked me to sign the guest book located on a stand by the door. I did so, writing in the names of those who had been on the cattle drive. I wonder if anyone has ever noticed that in that act fiction had been converted to fact. It is something I do every day. My life is fiction. That's a fact.

THE MOVIE AT THE END OF THE WORLD: TAKE ONE

All through the 1980s and even into the '90s, whenever I've given a reading (usually not from *The Last Cattle Drive* but from my novellas or short stories) there would be questions from the audience about the movie of *The Last Cattle Drive*. When was it going to be made? Was it true that Jack Nicholson was going to star? Or was it George C. Scott? Who would play Opal? Faye Dunaway? Meryl Streep? Who would play me (I was less the model for Leo than readers seemed to suppose, but privately I was hoping for Richard Dreyfuss).

Most authors don't mind being asked questions about writing or literature, but most of us wince when the literary success of our work is measured by nonliterary commercial success. And movies made from books are the most obvious indicators of such success. Also, some of the best movies are made from some of the worst books. That said, I of course knew that a movie staring Jack Nicholson was being planned and in fact had almost gotten made (see "*The Last Cattle Drive* Stampede"). When that project failed, there were other attempts to make the movie, most notably with Sean Connery as Spangler. But the Connery movie was to be re-titled and moved from Kansas to Montana. That prompted the following editorial published by the *Wichita Eagle Beacon* on March 10th, 1990.

BOO! Outrageous That The Last Cattle Drive Will Be Re-titled and Filmed in Montana

What could be worse than 20th Century Fox's plan to change the name of the movie version of *The Last Cattle Drive,* Robert Day's classic Kansas novel, to "Road Show"? Fox's plan to shoot the movie in Montana instead of Kansas this summer, that's what.

This makes about as much sense as calling the movie version of *Lonesome Dove,* Larry McMurtry's classic novel of the Plains, "Two Guys Who Want to Move to Montana" and filming it in New Jersey.

After all, Mr. Day's novel, published in 1977, is the tale of a crusty Western Kansas rancher who, appalled at modernity, decides to drive his cattle to the Kansas City stockyards instead of shipping them there by rail. The tale is told from the perspective of a young city slicker from Kansas City, who gets an education in what Kansas is really all about.

None of this matters, apparently. According to the Kansas Film Commission, actor Sean Connery is slated to star in the movie, and the producers want "mountain looks" to go with Connery; whatever that means. Well, excuuuuse us for not having any mountains. And excuse us, too, if we boycott the movie once it's released. Why shouldn't we? It won't have anything to do with Kansas.

As it turned out, the Sean Connery version of *The Last Cattle Drive* was not made in either Kansas or Montana. However, in the meantime there had been a lawsuit over the Nicholson/Hutton version of the movie that precipitated the bankruptcy of MGM. More on that in The Movie at the End of the World: Take Two. And on *City Slickers* in The Movie at the End of World: Take Three.

ANTHONY BURGESS AND MY CHANCELLORSHIP OF THE UNIVERSITY OF KANSAS

I met the writer Anthony Burgess in the early 1970s when I was a guest speaker at the University of Richmond. There was a lunch for Katherine Anne Porter (who had given me helpful advice about my writing when I was a student), the poet Richard Wilbur (who remains a friend after all these years), the great literary critic I. A. Richards, myself and Anthony Burgess—newly famous for, *Clockwork Orange*. I remember Burgess was smoking the cigars I later gave to the cattle buyer in the Kansas City stockyards at the end of *The Last Cattle Drive*.

Burgess and I liked each other immediately because (as Montaigne says about friendship) of who he was, and who I was. One result of our kinship was his vivid and lovely praise of my novel ("written in remarkably fine North American English") that has appeared in the many editions of the book, both in America and England.

Over the years, Burgess and I stayed in touch, and when he came to the University of Kansas to give a reading and meet with students and faculty he asked his hosts if arrangements might be made for me to join him. As it happened, I was then living in Western Kansas and so, along with my friend Ward Sullivan—who is rightly thought to be the model for Spangler in the novel—we drove the ranch pickup to Lawrence one afternoon after we had moved cattle that morning. The roundup had taken longer than we thought, so when we finally arrived at the Chancellor's House on Lilac Lane in the heart of the University's campus we probably still smelled of work. For sure we were not essence of lilacs blooming in the dooryard as we barged into the house. For sure we needed a drink. More than one. But there was no strong drink to be had.

We sat down with Burgess and a variety of professors and deans, all of us assembled on couches and comfortable Morris-like chairs. Someone offered us iced tea or hot coffee. Or water. I remember Burgess looking grim. Still we were pleased to see one another again, and we traded stories back and forth about our trips, what writers' paths we had crossed, and what books we were reading. Maybe there would be wine at dinner. Or at least tomato beer. That, too, was not to be the case.

In those days the fine biologist Del Shankel was the acting chancellor of the University of Kansas and there was a search being conducted to find a new Chancellor. That was the topic of discussion at dinner. What kind of chancellor would best suit the university. A scholar? A business man or woman? A leader from the world of politics? The deadline for applications and nominations was that very day. In a moment of levity, I nominated Anthony Burgess.

"I'll accept," said Burgess, "if I can get a drink."

"I second Mr. Burgess' nomination," said Ward, "but I need a drink as well."

"I don't think we have much by way of liquor in the place," said Del, who, after all, was just more or less house-sitting until the new chancellor was chosen. And besides, the university was no doubt officially dry at the time.

"We've got a bottle of Green Gables in the truck," said Ward. This was true. Before *The Last Cattle Drive* was published, Ward and I drank Jack Daniels Black, but because the characters drank Green Gables, we switched brands. Burgess, with his prodigious memory (he could recite most of *Ulysses*), knew right away the whiskey came from the novel. Ward went to the truck and brought back a full quart of Green Gables.

"Since we are drinking the fiction of whiskey from Bob's fact of a book," Burgess said as we started in on the bottle, "I withdraw my name to be chancellor of the University of Kansas and nominate Robert Day," Ward seconded the nomination. Now the professors and deans looked grim.

"You'll need to put that in writing before midnight," said Del. He seemed amused. "Do you want a piece of paper?"

"I'll use this napkin," said Burgess. We had put the Green Gables on an official University of Kansas paper napkin and some of the whiskey had run down the bottle so that the university's red and blue Jayhawk had become besotted.

"Curious creature," said Burgess looking at the Jayhawk. "One of your prairie birds, I expect. Are they good to eat?"

"They're imaginary," I said.

"More's the merrier!" said Burgess while writing my nomination on the napkin as if it were spoken, cartoon-like, by the Jayhawk. "I hereby nominate Robert Day to be Chancellor of the University of Kansas," he pronounced with a flourish, and handed, the napkin to Del Shankel.

I was not invited for an interview.

THE WRITING OF THE LAST CATTLE DRIVE

I wrote most of *The Last Cattle Drive* the summer of 1975 in a small farmhouse on the Smoky Hill River south of Gorham, Kansas. I did the first draft on a Hermes 10 typewriter I still have but now only use for letters and postcards. I revised the manuscript the following spring in Chestertown, Maryland. I reworked it again after it had been bought by G. P. Putnam in New York. Some of the rewriting I did on the typescript in my own hand which often I could not read. My guess is that over a third of the novel was not in its present form when I finished the initial draft. Writers are first of all (and finally as well) rewriters.

I remember that summer on the Smoky Hill was hot with the heat being broken now and then by violent storms ("thunderheads that climbed past twenty thousand feet"). At the time I was reading the novels and literary essays of Vladimir Nabokov and it is his remark that "weather is the first refuge of a sentimental writer" to which I allude at the opening of my chapter "Weather." I was also reading Andy Adams's *Log of a Cowboy* (which I did not understand was fiction until his cattle drive reached a nonexistent bog in Western Kansas) and *Huckleberry Finn*. Astute readers will spot fragments of sentences ("There is nothing more to write…") lifted from Mark Twain. And other elements as well.

Every morning after my writing I would drive the dirt roads of Western Kansas to take notes on the physiognomy of the land: limestone fence posts, creaking windmills, cottonwoods more in bunches than in groves. Doves in pairs on power lines. Grain trains. Stock racks in the beds of pickups, sometimes with a few head of low dollar steers heading to market; sometimes with a horse saddled and standing catty corner.

I had lived in the area in the late sixties when I was a teacher at Fort Hays State College and was more or less run out of both town and gown because of my antiwar activity as well as the production of my play *No Negro Problem in Hays.* (Among those attending the three packed performances of the play were KBI agents wearing ponchos, skimpy-brim hats and wing-tip shoes. I suppose they thought the ponchos were a good disguise).

While teaching and causing trouble, I worked for Ward Sullivan, and in so doing came to learn about cattle and ranching. But writing a novel about it made me focus on the precise nature of Western Kansas life. It wasn't the research that Tom Wolfe advocates for writers of fiction, but more noting the details of the daily life I had lived and that I now needed to make my story vivid. I am of the school of E. M. Forster who, when asked if he had researched *Passage to India,* said: "That wouldn't be fair, now would it?" Still, you don't want to have bogs in arid Western Kansas if you can help it, and you don't—as Eudora Welty once admitted to me she had done—make moons rise in the west.

Over the years I've gotten letters (and now e-mails) from readers of the novel telling me their favorite part and in turn asking for mine. Some readers like the moment at the start of the drive when Leo gets drunk and half falls off his horse. Others like the helicopter scene toward the end. Still others like the toast Spangler gives: "Friendships wane and friendships grow." For me, two moments stand out. One is when the tall man outside Lucas stops the herd and after some argument tells Spangler to kiss his ass, and Spangler says: "I don't stand in lines." The other is when Spangler sees the movie company filming the Western Kansas countryside and says, "I hope they leave the place the way they found it.... Nothing's the same after you take a picture of it." Here, he spoke for me.

In fact (as well as fiction), it was the movie *Paper Moon* they were making in and around Hays and Gorham when I was writing *The Last Cattle Drive*. Unlike the characters in the novel, I never saw any of the film crew. However, I once heard a public service announcement on the radio asking listeners to keep on the lookout for a poodle named Minnie that had been lost by one of the movie people. Ward named all such tiny, decorative dogs "bobcat bait." As Minnie probably was.

THE MOVIE AT THE END OF THE WORLD: TAKE TWO

One day I got in the mail a book titled *Fade Out* that was an account by Peter Bart of how MGM went bankrupt. A friend of mine had sent it with a note that I should read the chapter titled "Euphoria." I do judge books by their covers. And their blurbs. I have never read a book that was called "gripping." Nor one not written (nor read) by its author, usually some "celebrity." When I looked at *Fade Out* I could see no reason why I should spend even a tiny fraction of my life reading a story of how a movie company went broke. But I did. At least I read the chapter "Euphoria" as my friend had suggested.

According to Peter Bart, I am the principal reason MGM went belly up. The story is Hollywood's version of my fifteen minutes of fame. Apparently MGM needed a blockbuster movie to save it from financial collapse, and the movie of *The Last Cattle Drive* (retitled *Road Show*) was galloping to the rescue. Marty Ritt *(The Molly Maguires, The Front, Norma Rae)* was going to direct. Jack Nicholson and Timothy Hutton were the co-stars. Everything was "bankable": the director, the stars, the story. Even Kansas was bankable. At least Topeka, Kansas where—I am told—the city passed a special law saying that yes, MGM could drive a herd of cattle through downtown. The movie was a "GO" project if there ever was one.

Then Marty Ritt quit and Richard Brooks *(In Cold Blood)* took

over. Brooks quickly said the script was sick unto death of mad
cow disease and the whole premise of the novel was nuts and
stupid, and that was my fault. All of which led him to have a
heart attack high enough on the Richter scale of heart attacks
for MGM to cancel the picture (two days before it was to begin
shooting) and collect the insurance. But not so fast, said Timothy
Hutton, who smelled a fake heart attack. He sued. The rest of the
story is *Bleak House* peopled by swarms of sun-tanned California
lawyers. Finally, MGM has to pay. And goes belly up. The End. Of
my fifteen minutes of fame included.

WOMEN AND PROFANITY

I am told the book has a "tude" about women. At a reading I
gave in Berkeley, California, a woman in the audience asked me
how she could "cleave the attitudes of the characters from those
of the author." I was a little worried about that word "cleave";
it's what you do to the testicles of a bull calf to make a steer. Also,
she wanted to know, was it necessary to have so much profanity?
And finally, she asserted, you cannot hum the theme of the movie
Giant, nor say the word "shit" in seven syllables.

She was right about her final two complaints (it was the theme
of *High Noon* I had in mind, but somehow got as wrong as west
rising moons and bogs in Western Kansas). And as to "shit," the
best I can do is get five syllables out of it. I am told, however,
there are seven-syllable shit swearers out there. They must have
the lungs of Mario Lanza.

About the other complaints, it seems reasonable to point out
that it was a woman, Opal, who organized the drive, and who
solved the problem of what to do with the cattle once they had
been scattered—by men—across Kansas City. In the meantime,
the men in question (as Kansas's Carry Nation could have predicted) retire to Kelly's Tavern to piss and moan about the world.
And drink the night away.

I should also note that it is Spangler who observes to Leo that he won't fully appreciate women until he notices their faces instead of gawking at their breasts. I created Spangler as well as Leo. These points made, there is some truth in the observation that the book portrays the world of Western Kansas as a man's world. Just as there is some truth that Western Kansas and working cattle is a man's world. Wives are called "The Wife." Not "my wife Opal," nor simply "Opal." I have heard conversations among ranchers where I could not tell if the pronoun used referred to the man's horse, his pickup, or The Wife:

"How's yours this morning?"

"A little cranky, but after awhile, just fine. Yours?"

"The same."

Why should I cleave such scenes from their source? The first duty of a writer is not to lie about experience.

As to the profanity in *The Last Cattle Drive:* I like the story about the Western Kansas girl who went to Hollywood and became a starlet. One day she got out of a limousine and put her stylish high-heeled foot in a fresh pile of dog. "Oh, shit," she said. "I stepped in do-do."

A SEQUEL TO *THE LAST CATTLE DRIVE*; OR WHAT HAVE YOU WRITTEN SINCE?

I once wrote a long story using the characters of *The Last Cattle Drive* to see if they could live beyond the end of their book. They cannot. I placed them in Topeka, Kansas at a luncheon in their honor. They were served beef hearts. And tomato beer. Fancy women fussed about. There were speeches by political leaders who gave them "official recognition" (the first sign of "fatal misunderstanding" according to the American writer James Agee). But there was no action in the story. Ergo, no reaction. The story was as dead as a suburban dinner party where there is nothing to drink and you don't talk politics or religion.

Beyond that one failed story, I've not tried to write-or even much imagine—what a sequel might be. It can't be another drive because that would not only defeat the title of the book, and also what Leo writes two sentences before he rips off Mark Twain: "We know we can't do it again." Besides, I've had other stories to write, to wit: For a number of years I worked for the *Washington Post Sunday Magazine* as what the editor called "a chronic contributor." I also wrote for *Smithsonian* and *Forbes,* and even the old bland *Modern Maturity;* these days I contribute essays to The Prairie Writers Circle (some essays from all these publications are included elsewhere in this book). Beyond this work, I have been writing stories and novellas, some of them collected in a book titled *Speaking French in Kansas.* It is the novella (or what Katherine Anne Porter called The Long Story) that I like best. It is also the form that publishers, and thus probably the American public, like least. Who am I to tell that to my muse?

THE DEDICATION OF THE FIRST EDITION
"Virginia" was (and is) Virginia Wilds, my wife at the time I wrote the book. I have heard her say that living with me then was like living with a bear. Presumably not one in hibernation. "Edgar Wolfe" and "Edward Ruhe" (see tributes to each of these teachers elsewhere in this collection) were my professors; Edgar Wolfe taught me the value of precision in prose, Edward Ruhe showed me the breadth and depth of the literary life. Ward and Treva Sullivan are the models for Spangler and Opal; however, Ward once observed it might just as well be the other way around. His life was fiction, too. Opal was always pretty sure she could tell fact from fancy.

By the power invested in me to write "North American English" I now add to the original dedications Fred Whitehead, Perry Schwartz, and especially Kathryn Jankus Day (a.k.a. The Wife). How lovely to be able to do this.

THE MOVIE AT THE END OF THE WORLD: TAKE THREE:
CITY SLICKERS AND ART BUCHWALD

The reason these sections are titled The Movie at the End of World is because my agent once noted that so much money had been spent to not make the movie of *The Last Cattle Drive* that it would be the "end of the world" before it was finally made. It is also a title I've borrowed from the writer Tom McGrath. These are Hi-Signs from the Deities of Daily Living and Previous Literature, as we shall see in the following section. One assignment I had for the *Washington Post Magazine* was to write a piece on how much the movie *City Slickers* was indebted to *The Last Cattle Drive*. I am not an investigative reporter. The stories I wrote for the *Post Magazine* were mainly literary nonfiction, often about Kansas, but also about France, where I live part-time. In the case of *The Last Cattle Drive* and *City Slickers,* I was curious to know only what had been taken from my novel and used in the film. And I would learn this, not by traveling to Hollywood and doing interviews, but by watching the movie. Which I did.

I was struck, perhaps more than most people might be, at how *City Slickers* used aspects of my story: The modern-day cattle drive. The experienced rancher matched with a rookie hand. The calf that needs care. There were many dissimilarities as well. About this time I got a call from the same lawyers in California who had represented Timothy Hutton in his successful lawsuit with MGM. They wanted to know if I had seen *City Slickers* and did I want to bring legal action against the producers. To answer that question, and to add a back story to my piece for the *Post Magazine,* I flew to Martha's Vineyard to interview Art Buchwald, who was then suing Paramount Pictures concerning *Coming to America.* The conversation over hamburgers in Art's kitchen was long, funny, and finally precise. He had detailed the misery and money he had spent pursuing his own lawsuit.

"Do you think I should sue over *The Last Cattle Drive?*" I finally asked.

"It depends upon whether you want to be a writer for the next five years or a litigant," Art said. "Which is it?"

It turned out I wanted to be a writer.

THE STORY OF THE LAST CATTLE DRIVE

Two questions I have been repeatedly asked about *The Last Cattle Drive* are: Is it true? Or if not, where did I get the story?

By "true" I think people mean: Did the drive really take place? Put another way, is the book nonfiction? Or thinly disguised non-fiction, as if the annals of Kansas in the mid-seventies will show that a cattle drive went from somewhere north of Hays, Kansas into the Kansas City stockyard? The highways along which *The Last Cattle Drive* traveled, and the towns through which it went, are "real" therefore the drive itself was "real." All the author (one Robert Day, a.k.a. Leo Murdock) did was keep a journal, change a few names, and get it published as a novel. You might even be able to find evidence for this "reality" by checking the guest book of the Brookville Hotel restaurant. If the characters are listed there, that is prima facie evidence that the drive existed.

In fact, the drive was "real." I know because (to steal a line from the writer Truman Nelson) I made it up. But from where? From my life. Which is fiction.

The story of *The Last Cattle Drive* came from, as most of my stories do, a holy trinity of literary deities. The Deity of Previous Literature. The Deity of Daily Living. The Deity of Invention. These gods are not jealous gods to a writer—at least not to this writer. There are some stories I write that ask little of Daily Living. There are some that are deeply indebted to Previous Literature. But no story I have written—and certainly not *The Last Cattle Drive*—is bereft of any of these deities. It is the way art is made:

one part life, one part art, one part the energy of the artist—all mixed in some potent proportions as The Muse (the Mother of all Deities) dictates. It is T. S. Eliot's formula of "Tradition and the Individual Talent" with Invention as a catalyst.

A word about Invention. First, it is to be contrasted with Inspiration, which is a false deity. Those of us who write as a calling cannot trust our work to flourish though spasms of inspiration. Ask a Kansas rancher if he needs to be inspired to feed his cattle, check his fences, or break ice on the stock tanks after a hard freeze, and you'll get some gruff profanity. If you write a thousand words a day, you don't wait to see a white dove at sunrise to wire your fingers to your brain. My motto is: type, type-a-writer.

Then what is Invention? It is the leaps of imagination brought about by your own writing (or painting, or composing). In literature we see that Henry Fielding jumped into his invention of Parson Adams as he was riding in the otherwise dull carriage of Joseph Andrews not talking about politics or religion. Picasso attached bicycle handle bars to a bicycle seat and it became a bull's head. True, Picasso didn't get very far into his work when Invention made him leap, but that sometimes happens.

In *The Last Cattle Drive,* there are many moments of Invention: The baseball gear that Leo wears. The pheasants near Blackwolf (a mistaken invention as it turned out). Sissy. And there are moments when the Deity of Invention holds hands with Previous Literature: The scene where Leo is in the trailer toward the end of the drive and remembers (for the reader, of course) all that has happened before. That technique of knitting the book together I stole from Heinrich Boll's *The Clown.* Just as I stole the "This Book is for Jed" preface of *The Last Cattle Drive* (where the entire novel is coded—and that turns the book into a "document," the ultimate nonfiction "reality") from Nabokov's *Lolita.*

In the end I am amused (and mused) to think that a Western American cowboy novel has stuffed into it not only my red jeep (from the daily living of my callow youth), but hunks and chunks of German literature, American Mississippi River literature, and a previous cattle drive story all dancing *ensemble* with a Russian author's nymphet in her "circular skirt and scanties." I wonder what Spangler would have thought had he met her. Or Leo, for that matter. My, my.

"I SHALL TRY TO TELL THE TRUTH, BUT THE RESULT WILL BE FICTION." — KATHERINE ANNE PORTER

There is nothing more to write.

"Siesta"

Author's Note:
Parts of Their Nights

These three small essays (for that is what they are, not "pieces") are my testimony that a literary life (mine at least) is laced with a debt to others. It is a pleasing debt to be sure, and it feels good to honor it.

Nabokov

There is a National Educational Television film in which Vladimir Nabokov is asked what he thinks of his reading public, and he says that his main audience (his only audience) is himself and Vera, his wife. Then he pauses and says he is often pleased and amused by the cards and letters he gets from all over the world, from remote places such as Kansas, and that these readers have sometimes taken from his work the same pleasure he had when he composed it. I like to think Nabokov is speaking of me.

In the early 60s I took off a spring semester from my studies at the University of Kansas in order to "read." That was fashionable in those days, especially if you were a serious literary student.

The idea was that you would read the writers the literary departments at the university were not teaching: B. Traven and Powers, R. S. Thomas and Philip Larkin, Amos Tutuola and Chinua Achebe, Frank O'Connor and Brendan Behan. And Vladimir Nabokov.

I lived in a farmhouse south of Lawrence, toward Lone Star Lake. The house and farm were owned by the Widow Dunn, a feisty woman who would stop by every day to "check up on things." (She wondered aloud why I wasn't in school more). The agreement I had struck with Mrs. Dunn was that I would do a certain amount of work each week in order to pay part of the rent. It was dollar-an-hour work, and most of it was tacking old barbed-wire fence back into very old (and consequently very tough) Osage Orange fence posts. If you were lucky you could find a split in the wood and start there—unless you were Mrs. Dunn, in which case you drove in the staple anywhere without any trouble at all.

I recall all this because that spring when I didn't go to school I also tried not to work much for Mrs. Dunn, and I took to hiding in a back room, a copy of *Pale Fire* or *Lolita* with me, until Mrs. Dunn assumed I wasn't home or was "with someone," as she once put it.

Reading those novels (I was 19 at the time) was a little like driving in staples: I did not see point to it, except to get it done—to be well-read; and it was difficult work. There was, however, a certain pleasure to be taken particularly in *Pale Fire* at finding passages where my efforts paid off—where I understood the pleasure the author was taking in his writing. But on the whole those books eluded me, and I recall more clearly my reading of J. D. Salinger's *Catcher in the Rye*, and Holden Caulfield's theory of literary criticism: A good book will make you want to call the author. Salinger, it turned out, could not be reached by phone, and it did not occur to me to call Vladimir Nabokov. Now, when I want to, I can't.

Years later (after I'd read all of his novels and much of his other writing) I was bewildered—and still am—by the criticism that Nabokov is a writer of sheer technique and style, whose final achievements would not include much of an ability to say anything about the pleasures and pains of being human.

Nabokov is a cold writer, I'd read in the literary journals. He is mostly strategy, I was told by one of my teaching colleagues. He is arch; he is arrogant. He is brutal; he is ascetic. He writes without concern for his characters and moves them around like so many chess pieces—or pins them wriggling to a board like a butterfly.

His novels burn without warmth. I never thought any of this to be true, and even in my initial difficulty with reading *Pale Fire* and *Lolita* I did not think Nabokov heartless.

He seems to me a nostalgic writer who used his technical skills and craft to keep his characters and his books from drifting into sentimentality. What shows in all of his work is a strong affection for art—the art of making good sentences, splendid paragraphs, wonderful novels. He loved his art. When, at the end of *Lolita* his character Humbert writes: "I am thinking of aurochs and angels, the secret of durable pigments, prophetic sonnets the refuge of art. And this is the only immortality you and I may share, my Lolita." I know that while Humbert may be writing about his love, Nabokov is writing about his book by the same name.

The affection for art, for what Nabokov once called "aesthetic bliss," does not mean he is without insight into human nature. I find the genius of the author is in his sense of proportions and design, so that what is amusing and what is poignant is tumbled together in a way that reminds us of our own lives.

Well, he is dead now. I think it was Hemingway writing about the death of Conrad who said he was sorry he had read all of Conrad because now there would be nothing new of his to read. I know how Hemingway felt. I have saved back nothing of Vladimir Nabokov's. It is there to read again, and that will be great pleasure, but it is not the same as having the writer alive and well, and working on something new in his room in Montreux, Switzerland.

It took me quite a while to read all his novels and stories, and perhaps I should be glad that I did not get on with him too well that first spring south of Lawrence, the Widow Dunn trying to flush me out for work. The truth is I didn't read another Nabokov book for years. I was teaching in western Kansas and living in a ranch house miles from town. For some reason a publisher sent me a free copy of *The Defense*—a story of a gentle and awkward man who plays championship chess, and who falls in love in many ways, and who dies. What a wonderful book, I recall thinking. It started me up again and soon I was rereading *Pale Fire* and *Lolita*, and later *The Gift, Bend Sinister, Speak Memory, Mary* and *King, Queen, Nave.*

But by my memory it was after reading *The Defense* that I wrote to Vladimir Nabokov to tell him (à la Holden Caulfield) that I liked that book and others, and in what ways I did. I wrote him in care of his publisher, and I have no idea if he ever got it. There was no reply. But when I saw him peering at me out of that National Educational Television film to say that he was amused at the letters he got from such "remote places as Kansas" I thought he must be speaking of me. I wish I'd called.

It is in that same film that Nabokov speaks of the pleasure of writing—a pleasure he says comes from first finding the correct word or phrase or detail—the one that had until its discovery eluded him. Beyond that, he goes on to say, there is the diabolical thrill of having "cheated creation by creating something yourself." He has done it, I think—cheated creation, and his epitaph is that like Lolita, his immortality is safe within the refuge of art.

I Look Out For Ed Wolfe

Being Twelve Notes on University Days, the Craft of Fiction, Coincidence, the Mind's Eye, Significant Details, Multiple Sclerosis, One Teacher plus One Character from Fiction, All on a Snowy Winter Afternoon in a Now Defunct Campus Building and Written With Correct Spelling and Punctuation, plus a Modicum of Sentimentality for Which the Author Does Not Apologize.

1. The Nature of Titles. The Nature of Coincidence.

One of the things I learned from Ed Wolfe, my writing teacher at the University of Kansas, is that you can't copyright titles. I could have called this essay "Of Education," or *War and Peace,* or *Casablanca.* I could have called it "Penny Lane"—a song that was popular during the years I learned about titles and other literary matters from a man whose name happened to be Ed Wolfe—as in the famous short story by Stanley Elkin "I Look Out For Ed Wolfe."

Coincidence, my Ed Wolfe will teach his students, is one of the energies of fiction. It turned out my Ed Wolfe and Stanley Elkin met each other one sad day, and that years later I met Stanley Elkin on another sad day; these coincidences are the rough stuff of life, but more on that later. For now, back to the present/past: You were first in print, Mr. Elkin, but I hereby exercise my muse-given right as an author to be a literary thief. I too look out for Ed Wolfe.

2. An Old Campus Building. Harris Flora and John Donne.

I am sitting in Fraser Hall, now defunct, the victim of some dreary university administration that thought it would look better as a pile of rocks than as the aging ivy twin tower building it was— and still is in my imagination, where I have held both Ed Wolfe and his Fraser Hall office like a hologram against a practical and efficient world. *Imagine the specifics of the objects you are describing*, Ed Wolfe will teach me. *Imagine them in detail.*

   Part of whatever ability I have to express what I imagine about such places as Fraser Hall I owe to Ed Wolfe. It is not enough to have talent, he has told me (although he's never told me I have talent), and it is not enough to want to be a writer (although he knows I want to accomplish that)—what I need is a sense of duty to the craft. And patience with myself would help (I have told him at our previous meeting if I don't get published in the *New Yorker* by the time I am twenty-two, I'm going to stop writing and take up a job with the Lawrence, Kansas, police force.) And finally, Ed Wolfe will note again: *an eye for detail is where honesty in fiction rests.*

   Beyond these lessons, Ed Wolfe suggests I might also want to do plenty of reading. Long before Saul Bellow made his famous remark, Ed Wolfe has been teaching his students that writers should be readers moved to emulation. *Learn to write dialogue from Ring Lardner*, Ed Wolfe has said to me. Since I'd never heard of Ring Lardner I kept my mouth shut and later bought a Scribner's copy of *Haircut and Other Stories*. My library of books as texts to learn the craft of writing grows larger than my literary course library. It is a good beginning.

   Ed Wolfe, like E. M. Forster before him, thought of literary tradition not so much as a great long historical queue of English authors, but rather as a round dinner table where we all ate together and talked books.

Pull up a chair, Mr. Donne and Miss Austen. That's Bob Day and Harris Flora sitting across from you. Why don't you read your work aloud and talk. Mr. Day, Mr. Flora, you listen and learn. It is through such *en famille* literary meals that I have begun the process of becoming a writer.

By the time I am sitting across from Ed Wolfe in Fraser Hall this singular snowy winter afternoon I have read my Ring Lardner. As well, I have learned from Katherine Anne Porter, William Stafford, J. D. Salinger, Jack London, Vladimir Nabokov, Ed Wolfe, Robert Service, and Jane Austen.

Harris Flora, my friend and fellow student writer in those days, has been instructed to learn from Dos Passos, Anderson, and the English novelist Meredith. Harris and I have been trading what we have learned over lunch at the Gaslight Tavern. Ed Wolfe is teaching us how to teach ourselves: he knows that, we don't. It is called dramatic irony.

3. God Knows We Are All Unbearably Sentimental.

God knows we are all unbearably sentimental about our college education. Our American minds are full of guitar songs, wine bottles with candles in them, old Studebakers, the back seats of old Studebakers, good friends past and forgotten with the rest, campus dogs and ducks, and the hallways and staircases of old stone buildings. I sometimes wonder how the chairs and benches of our college memories can be sat upon at all they seem so precious and painterly.

Is Fraser Hall really all that worn and splendid? And my teacher, Ed Wolfe? Is he as instructive as this memoir makes him out to be?

Or are they both wasted space: a campus building that when you cut away large swatches of the ivy on its sides reveals to the prying eyes of the engineer witch doctors (who knew "it" all along) large "significant" cracks placidly making their way among the stones; and what of Ed Wolfe, an "Associate" Professor (remember Elizabeth Taylor nagging Richard Burton in *Who's Afraid of Virginia Woolf*: "Associate Professor, Associate Professor") with but one novel under his belt, no Ph.D., and a slow and deliberate fashion of speech that is at odds with the impatient generation he is teaching? What to make of the long pauses between your questions and his answers? What to the prying eyes of academic promotion engineers does Ed Wolfe reveal?

4. Mecurical, Mercurial, and Nina Wolfe.

Ed Wolfe's Fraser Hall office slants toward the east exterior wall of the building, and when you visit him you sit in the only other chair in the room—a swivel chair of the professor whose desk is near the door but who is seldom there. The chair you sit in, the desk where you sit, the book shelves that rise up the wall in front of the desk, all combine to give you a feeling of importance: it is the seed of pretentiousness, and it is difficult when you are nineteen and have the week before just written your first really long story—it is difficult not to swivel and rock back in *your* office chair, as if you were debating in your mind the influence of Sartre's work on your own.

   Ed Wolfe doesn't seem to notice: he points out you've yet to spell "suburban" correctly, and that it took "both of them" (by that he means that his wife, Nina, who is bedridden with multiple sclerosis, has been consulted), to understand that "mecurical" was "mercurial." And then there are some matters of punctuation. Is it impossible for me to learn where in a quoted question the question mark is to be placed? So much for Sartre.

5. Cornucopia Finance Corporation and the Mind's Eye.

The Ed Wolfe that Stanley Elkin looks out after is a telephone bill collector who loses his job because he's too aggressive in collecting his accounts for Cornucopia Finance Corporation.

"You're in trouble. It means a lien. A judgement. We've got lawyers. You've got nothing. We'll pull the furniture the hell out of there. The car. Everything...If you're short, grow. This is America." His boss fires him.

Stanley Elkin's Ed Wolfe takes his severance pay, adds in some money from selling his clothes and car, empties his checking and savings account, so that added together his net worth is $2,479.03—all of which he accumulates in cash with the idea of making it through the rest of his life. In the end, Elkin's Ed Wolfe throws it all away: one night both life and money get tossed onto the damp dirty floor of a dreary tavern. So much for the American Dream.

Stanley Elkin's Ed Wolfe and my Ed Wolfe have little in common: true; they both play handball (my Ed Wolfe was a champion), but beyond that nothing. Still, there is something magical about their mere coincidental existence, if not their antithesis; it is as if all concerned (the two Ed's and the two authors) have conspired to make fiction fluctuate between reality and the hologram of the mind's eye—between the real snow I see falling outside my Ed Wolfe's office window and the snow we see in the glass ball of winter scenes.

6. Wallace Stevens and Snow.

Fraser Hall is old and drafty, a fire trap, and full of wasted space. "Wasted space" was a great sin to the university administrators who never bothered to look out their windows at the broad sweep of prairie around them. Looking out of Ed Wolfe's Fraser Hall office window I can see east twenty miles down the Kansas River Valley toward Eudora and Kansas City. Even in the huge brush strokes of the panorama I can see the details of small farming roads and tear-drop shaped ponds among the larger lovely space. It is blue outside. Blue and gray and white. It is winter; it is snowing. And, as Wallace Stevens has predicted in a previous class, it is going to snow.

7. Some Events Narrated Out of Sequence.

Because he cares for his wife with the same combination of duty and affection that he cares for words, Ed Wolfe knows a great deal about multiple sclerosis. At some point Ed Wolfe meets Stanley Elkin, the unwitting author of "I Look Out For Ed Wolfe." At that meeting Ed Wolfe notices certain symptoms in Stanley Elkin (having to do with the eyes) that are precursors to multiple sclerosis. Ed Wolfe tells Stanley Elkin what he knows.

Years later in San Francisco I meet Stanley Elkin in a hotel lobby. I do not know the story about Ed Wolfe telling Stanley Elkin what he has told him. Nor of its prophetic truth. I say, "My teacher was Ed Wolfe at the University of Kansas. Do you know him?"

"Yes," says Stanley Elkin, and when he gets up to greet me I see that he has a cane and that he is shaking. "He was my teacher too." Mr. Elkin sits back down and turns to his left as if searching for a window out of which he can look. I do not know what any of this means, but I sense I have walked into an office where I should not be. I back away without saying anything more. It was not all that long ago that I learned this part of the story.

8. What I Am Writing.

I see I am writing these sentences to discover what I think about these matters, just as I am sitting in Ed Wolfe's Fraser Hall office to discover what I have written. There are twenty-five years between my two selves. By what name is that space to be called? If it is a question, should I try to answer it?

9. The Sentimental Education of Young Writers at the Gaslight Tavern.

In those days, before the boom in college Creative Writing Programs and all the modern techniques that go with them, which, I want to confess up front, I am as guilty as the next writer/ teacher of spreading, you learned your craft not so much from "the writing program" as from your teacher—and you learned writing not so much in the class room as from the other end of the log. In Ed Wolfe's case this process began when he returned your story—usually a week or so after you had turned it in. What you got back was an annotated edition of your work with a long, hand-written survey of its accomplishments and faults.

The survey would start on the back of your final page and proceed from your story's conclusion toward your story's beginning. You'd find Ed Wolfe's account was complete with samples of what you might have written; whole sections of your story would be reworked, complete with dialogue and narration. Often when you'd turn your story's pages over from Ed Wolfe's writing to yours you'd discover that his comments matched page for page the very text he was rewriting. It was a twice-told tale, and it was enormously flattering. For reasons I cannot explain, this process did not violate your sense of artistic honor—which at age nineteen could easily be violated in a thousand small ways.

Harris Flora and I would take our Ed Wolfe/Flora/Day stories over to the Gaslight Tavern and read aloud what we had written. Is it to our credit (and I think it is) that we wondered then if energy for Ed Wolfe's own fiction was being spent on ours, that for every sentence he rewrote for us, he used up a sentence he might have written for himself? It was the kind of simple equation you believe in when you are young and talking about literature and drinking beer. What does it say about me that I believe it even now?

At the end of Ed Wolfe's survey you'd get your grade and a small drawing of a wolf. Well, sort of a wolf. It was a most benign wolf, and it seemed to have been drawn out of the very script that Ed Wolfe used to critique your work, almost as if letters that might have gone into yet another rewritten sentence had found themselves rearranged into a modest-size drawing of a mildly amused and harmless wolf, teeth and all.

10. The Slant of Ed Wolfe's Office. The Nature of Fiction. Duty.

The desk chair where I am sitting in Ed Wolfe's office has wheels, and over the course of your conversation with Ed Wolfe you have a tendency to roll downhill toward him, which turns out to be necessary because the longer Ed Wolfe talks, the softer he speaks. The important criticisms worthy of a good story are put very softly and near the end of your conversation, so it is a good sign if by the end of your meeting you wind up more or less bumping chairs with Ed Wolfe. It is a bad sign if you don't spend enough time in the chair to slide very far downhill. Your progress down the slope of Ed Wolfe's Fraser Hall office is something of a barometer of how well you have written. This afternoon I won't make much progress toward the window where my teacher is framed in the fading light.

"I have decided," Ed Wolfe says, "to return to an old system of reading your stories." Here he holds up the front page of my work. I can see even in the gathering darkness (the office lights seemed never to be turned on) that my great opening scene is heavily penciled. Ed Wolfe turns the story around to show me that there is nothing written on the back of the final page. That is not a good sign. The longer the critique of your work, like the longer roll you make in the office, the better your story is. One page of rewriting is no compliment at all. There was that folklore/rumor about the student who wrote so badly that Ed Wolfe wrote nothing in return. In the gloom of Ed Wolfe's office I am beginning to feel like someone who has become a character in a fiction not of his own making.

"You need," Ed Wolfe says, "to have some respect for the spelling of the English language and the punctuation of English sentences. I have corrected the first page. I have not read further. You can correct the rest. When you have, return the story to me and we shall talk." He hands me my story and leans back in his chair and puts his left elbow on the window ledge.

Oddly, I notice for the first time that at the edge of window along the sill there is snow blowing in: a small drift is collecting just where Ed Wolfe's elbow is resting. I am wondering if I will ever be able to use in a short story what I am seeing: how to describe this thin, light crescent of snow assembling itself inside the window of a professor's office. How to match that up against the feeling of the weight my story makes in my hands as I realize there is a lifetime of work to do and yet I don't know what a lifetime of anything means?

"Words," Ed Wolfe says leaning away from the window, "words are the first element in writing to admire. There are other things to like about writing. Sentences. Plot. Character. But you must start with an affection for words." He pauses and turns his chair away from me so that we are both looking out his window. "What are you saying about a word when you don't bother to know how to spell it? What are you saying about a word if you abbreviate it? Cinn. M.S. If you do that, who's to say if you'll describe anything correctly? Or admire the fullness of it? The snow outside my window. The color of shadows. The way the snow comes in through the crack and onto the sill." He turns back to face me. "The first detail of fiction is the word."

11. A Question of Fiction in Search of an Answer

Suburban, mercurial. The crescent of snow along the edge of the
window. The hologram in my mind of Fraser Hall that is only lit by
the dimming afternoon light coming through Ed Wolfe's window.
The glee and sorrow of coincidence. The flux of life and fiction.
The Gaslight Tavern. Harris Flora. Ed Wolfe. Ed Wolfe. Stanley
Elkin. The table where we all sit, words and question marks alike
pulling up chairs along with Ring Lardner and John Donne and
asking out loud, how do we know one another? And what will
become of our fellowship? What indeed? If that is a question, do I
have to answer it? I think I do. Even if it takes a lifetime of work.

12. "I Look Out For Ed Wolfe," a story by Stanley Elkin.

I look out for Ed Wolfe.

Parts of Their Night:
An Elegy for Our Professors

He never seemed to know what kind of car he owned nor what sports season it was. On the other hand, he always seemed to know what nasty business Richard Nixon was up to, or what new Bergman film was being released.

When I first met him in 1959 it was football season and he drove a rusting blue 1952 wrap-around-windshield, four door Pontiac. I remember the car not only because as a freshman from the suburbs you knew everything about cars in those days, but because Professor Ruhe—for that's who he was to me as the teacher of my freshman English class—because Professor Ruhe and I had spent nearly an hour late one afternoon trying to find the auto in question before it quietly dawned on him that he'd walked to campus that day.

"Maybe it's in the parking lot by the football stadium," I recall saying about halfway through the search-in-progress.

"*Virgin Spring* is playing this evening," Professor Ruhe said by way of response. "Eight P. M. showing. I hope they don't cut it."

Why he had offered me a ride home after our class, I don't remember. I do remember that I could have gotten back to my dorm under my own steam in plenty of time for supper, but now the matter seemed in doubt. Hunger in a young man is rarely metaphysical. Still, out of some kind of respect that is difficult to rename these days, in the nineteen fifties you didn't abandon a professor in search of his car—no matter how much your stomach growled.

By now we'd walked through three KU parking lots, down two side streets, and were heading more or less at random across the campus lawns toward the campanile and, beyond the duck pond, my dorm. Our search was apparently not along the horizontal and vertical grid you use when on patrol for lost boy scouts; instead we seemed to be going over a landscape of verbal paths in Professor Ruhe's mind, some set of associations that formed a map all its own. On these cerebral walkways we'd already come upon Blake and Johnson, taken a left turn out of the parking lot at Pope and Swift, and trudged up a hill toward Hardy and Ernest Dowson. It was near the campanile that we came upon Bergman, *Virgin Spring*, and Richard Nixon.

Here and there a few students were walking toward the Student Union for supper. In the distance a brass pep band was blaring a fight song. The afternoon was gold turning to red. Across the duck pond I could see my dorm: a stacked hotel of square room windows.

"What color is your car?" I asked; I was on the lunatic fringe of starvation. Early on he had told me we were looking for something "General Motors." Years later, after I was no longer his student and had become his friend I watched in placid amazement as—with the certainty of a stockbroker getting into his Silver Bullet Porsche—he climbed into a car he had sold two years before only to be foiled in his attempt to drive it off because his "something Japanese" keys would not fit the lock of his previously owned "something Ford."

"Green," he said. "Green."

"Green?" I said.

"Blue," he said.

"Blue?" I said.

"I suppose they'll cut it badly," he said. I had no idea what he was talking about.

"Yes," I said.

"It's Richard Nixon's tribe at work again," he said. And here Professor Ruhe shook his head, pursed his lips and let something like a rumble of distant thunder. Over the years those of us who became his friends knew that sound as the precursor to an inevitable rant about one of his permanent angers: censorship, materialism, suburban ethics, Richard Nixon, teacher evaluation forms, and what he called "the corporate university." The disgust of ancient freethinkers seemed to echo in his thunder; the dismay of American civil libertarians shook with his head. It was as if he might keep such nonsense at bay with contempt and derision. He was largely an innocent man.

"James Agee," he said after a moment as we stood there in the bulging shadows of the campus buildings that were turning the afternoon into evening, "James Agee wrote that official acceptance is a sure sign of fatal misunderstanding. And Mozart wrote that he'd spent his life searching for notes that loved one another." We learned that our professor's rant could be calmed by a self-administered dose of James Agee or Mozart, not to mention hundreds of other splendid author, painters, and composers who formed the matrix of his life and were a delight and balm to his soul. A little Mozart went a long way in his various battles with Richard Nixon.

"What do you think?" he asked me.

I was eighteen. I was from the suburbs. I didn't know James Agee or Bergman or Blake or Johnson or *Virgin Spring*—whoever she was. I knew how to throw a curve ball to the outside corner of the plate and how to set a pick for a cutting guard; I knew Ozzie and Harriet were married off television as well as on; and I knew that General Eisenhower had been President of the United States since the beginning of real time. It was 1959. Football fall, 1959.

We all had a lot to learn. We were all largely innocent. I didn't know what to think.

"Hello," he says. It is decades later. Ed Ruhe—for that is who he is to me now—Ed Ruhe has answered the phone in that half-hectic voice we who were his students know.

"The *Atlantic Monthly* calling," I say. He plays along.

"What can I do for you?"

"We need a piece on Richard Nixon as the emblem of ethics in government," I say. "Five thousand words."

"I might get five hundred words," he says through his laugh. "Like a freshman blue book." In my mind's eye I can see his head shaking in the old wrath; then it stops. I ask him how he is.

"Fine," he says. "I've been thinking about Flannery O'Connor. And you?"

"I've been thinking about William Stafford's poetry," I say.

"How firm and sure it is," he says. "*Pray for the frozen dead at Yellow Knife / These words we send are becoming parts of their night.*"

"Yes," I say.

"I've been thinking about the revelations in O'Connor," he says. "Those visions."

"Astounding, aren't they?" I say.

We are silent for a moment because he needs to catch his breath. I find myself thinking about teachers: good teachers, bad teachers, great teachers. It's a television topic these days. But I am thinking that my best teachers were always a bit zany around the social edges and no doubt maladjusted at the core, as if wounded by what they'd seen near the bone of *King Lear*, *The Rhyme of the Ancient Mariner*, *The Seventh Seal*, or *Mahler's Ninth*. These professors all had something I think of as dignity. How this grew out from their character and into their physiognomy and fixed me with its authority I am sure I know: they loved their teaching subjects above all else, and it showed. It showed on Ed Ruhe more than most.

"Remember those teacher evaluation forms the students filled out on you?" I say.

"They wrote I had annoying personal mannerisms," he says. I hear faint thunder. Absurdly, I am recalllng the time he taped Rilke poems to the dashboard of his car so he could learn German as he drove around town. We watched him motor through stop signs on his way to fluency.

"What are you reading?" I ask.

"Joyce Cary," he says. "You know we never gave Bill Stafford an honorary degree. What madness is that?"

"He doesn't have any oil wells," I say.

"Poets don't have oil wells," he says. "We have to do better."

"I think we do," I say.

It occurs to me that over the years most of our battles have been lost, but I don't say this. Instead we trade a few stories: it is the pleasure of good friends, this telling of the same tales over and over again as if by so doing we can weave a tapestry against mortality.

"I've been watching *Walkabout*," he says. "And practicing my colloquial language."

"What colloquial language?"

"You know," he says, "how the students complained on my evaluations that I didn't speak their language, so I'm practicing: 'Milton uses epic similes, *man!* Sam Johnson is the English Dictionary, *wow, really!* Blake gets in your face, *man!*'"

"You'll be the teacher of the decade," I say. "You'll get an award. Official acceptance."

Again a moment of silence while he catches his breath, then laughs.

"I've got to go," he says. Through the phone I hear that someone has come into the back of his apartment; perhaps a former student like myself. We stop in on him these days.

"See you later," I say.

"You know what Auden said?" he asks.

"What?"

"That talk about literature should be filled with insight and advocacy. What do you think?"

"Auden's right," I say. I am thinking of Bill Stafford's poems, of James Agee, of notes that love one another, of *Lear*, of insight and advocacy, of visions, and of walks you take in your life with Johnson and Milton and Bergman as companions. Before he hangs up, Ed asks me to remember him to some former students.

"I've got to go," he says.

"Good-bye," I say.

"Good-bye," he says.

Good-bye: So say we all.

Author's Note:
The Prairie Writers' Circle

All of the essays in this section I wrote for—or because of—my association with the Prairie Writers Circle, a group of authors brought together by Wes Jackson of the Land Institute. They were republished by newspapers all over the country, and many of them appeared on web sites such as *Counter Punch*, and by necessity had to be limited to about 750 words.

"The Committee To Save the World" was written for the Land Institute's Conference on Ignorance with its theme: *Since we're billlons of times more ignorant than knowledgeable, why not go with our long suit and have an ignorance-based world view?* Contrarian to a fault, I took the view that "everything is known." The essay was later published in *New Letters*.

"Robinhood's Barn"

The Scholar and Artist Homestead Act for 21st-Century America

I have an idea. How about we repopulate the rural areas of America with poets and painters and scholars? And oboe players who want to practice in the solitude of the High Plains?

My thinking is that we get a Rich Somebody's Foundation to buy up semi-ghost towns with the idea of repairing the abandoned houses, cleaning the lots, turning on the street lights, and then inviting a sonnet writer from Brooklyn to Petrarch away in peace for a few months with a morning coffee pot perking in the kitchen and coyotes howling at the edge of town at night. It would do both the town and the poet good.

What's so funny?

My wife and I live like this. She's a painter working with glee and oils in a rebuilt chicken shed we had pulled onto our property in Bly, Kansas. There is no Bly, Kansas. I'm not going to tell you where we live. Only that we live in a town like Bly. A lovely, more than half-abandoned town on the High Plains with wild turkeys walking West Dirt Street and dove roosts in the cottonwood trees.

We've got fine neighbors. Do they think we're strange because my wife doesn't make paintings of windmills and that I don't write cowboy poetry for Hallmark Cards—much less run cattle for a living? Yup. Do they like us and help us? Our neighbors are the ones who set up my wife's chicken shed. It's been great fun.

By my counting there are half a dozen houses in Bly that could be bought and repaired. Maybe more if you add the ones that aren't for sale but are falling down and might be for sale if you could find the owner. And there might be 10 lots or so onto which you could move in houses from the country.

What the Rich Somebody's Foundation does is buy these properties and hire local contractors to put them in good shape. Then the foundation establishes a trust run by the local banks, and the trust pays for the upkeep of the houses. It wouldn't be much over the years. Oboe players don't do much damage to property.

When it is all settled about the money and the trust, and when the windows of the houses are washed and the floors swept clean, and the squirrels and the pack rats have been run out of the attics, you print a Homestead flyer for the rest of America.

Free House In Kansas.

But not free to everybody. And not free forever.

I imagine a scholar who needs six months to finish a book on Carry Nation that is difficult to write because there's no place in his high rise to walk between paragraphs. Writers need a place to walk between paragraphs. Montaigne says his mind was never busy unless his feet were. We've got paragraph breaks all over Bly.

I imagine a potter who arrives from Denver one spring morning with a load of wheels, a kiln and buckets of clay, and by the next day you can hear the wheel spinning as you walk down Middle Dirt between paragraphs. Then a few days later in the Bly Co-op on the edge of town (where the Committee to Save the World meets over coffee) they are talking:

"Did you see we got ourselves a woman potter this time?"

"My favorite was the bagpipe player."

"Is it true she'd play her bagpipes all by her lonesome down the creek where Cody keeps his goats?"

"It is."

"I liked the poet. He didn't seem to do anything but he didn't brag about it."

"Cody claims the music was good for his goats."

What's so funny?

I imagine my wife in her chicken shed looking out the windows to the south, where she can see rows of pots being set out in the October sunshine by a woman from Denver who has done lovely work over the summer and who, later in the day, will make the rounds here in Bly to thank everybody for how kind they have been, and invite them over to see the pots, and to pick one for themselves as a gift for their kindness. And we will all gather together and tell stories about the bagpipe player and how her music was good for Cody's goats.

I like my idea.

Ode to Red

"Our grass will grow in the streets of your towns."
American Indian prophecy

I am sitting in the high school gym in Brewster, Kan., watching a girls' basketball game. A friend of mine and I have driven 40 miles from Atwood to Brewster because there is a regional basketball tournament and my friend's son is a star player. In half an hour he will have a very good night, leading his team to victory with a blizzard of three-point shots. Until then we are killing time and saving center court seats by watching the girls' game.

I have become fascinated by the play of a point guard. The crowd calls her "Red." "Go, Red," they yell when she gets the ball. "Get 'em, Red. Go." She is very good.

Out here in towns like Atwood and Oberlin and St. Francis—all who have teams in the Brewster tournament—the population is declining. No news there. It's been going that way for 50 years. Stores are boarded up. Houses are abandoned. Lots are vacant, some with cars or trucks or trailers left behind as the owners moved on to Denver or Kansas City. Nobody's coming back.

Eight- and even six-man football is now played at some small-town high schools. It's sad, but it's either that or drop the sport.

Nobody wants to do that. Sports give everybody something to cheer for on winter nights. The town of Brewster is packed with pickups from hundreds of square miles of the High Plains.

"Go, Red, go." I love it. "Red" was my nickname when I was her age and running up and down the hardwoods. I thought of myself as Bob Cousy. Not that I could dribble behind my back, or hit his one-hand running set shot. Nor did I have much speed. Being Bob Cousy was just a dream I had for myself.

But the "Red" I am watching can dribble behind her back. She is fast. And she has a shot that is better than any shot I ever had, and better than most of the boys with whom I played. She can also pass—sometimes with such skill and speed it catches her teammates unaware. When that happens, and the ball sails out of bounds, Red claps her hands—not in exasperation with her teammate, or even at herself for throwing the ball too quickly, but as if to reset herself, now on defense, the game coming back her way: She picks up her girl with an eye to forcing a turnover, or stealing the ball, or blocking a shot. Get 'em, Red.

Screens. Give and go. Top of the key. Fast break. In the paint. I remember the language of the game as it was taught to me. I remember as well how the girls played it in those days: half court. A defensive three and an offensive three. They didn't cross the center line. I suppose the thinking was that girls couldn't run the full court without fainting. Or without breaking a sweat—which none of them wanted to do. That's not true of Red. She plays the game with glee, as do the other girls on her team. Up and down the court they go: picks, screens, fast breaks—plus dribbling and passing and shooting with either hand.

As I watch her play, I think: If there is six-man football on the High Plains, won't it follow that there soon will be three-man basketball? Three-on-three we used to call it. Or two-on-two. The number of boys who showed up to play on a Saturday afternoon divided in half. Won't it sooner or later come to that out here? One-on-one. Me and Red for the High Plains Basketball Championship.

She blocks my Bob Cousy running set shot and fast breaks for an easy lay-up. I miss a hook. She hits a jump shot from the top of the key. I am trailing by 10. Red passes to herself and runs behind me to get it—then full court through the paint. Another lay-up. From the bleachers an old rancher cheers, "Go, Red, go." The clock is counting down. Outside the shortgrass prairie is coming up in the streets of Brewster.

Red makes one last shot.

"Garcia"

Talk to Strangers and Stop On By

At the Library of Congress in 1994 there was a tribute to William Stafford, the American poet who, in 1970, had been what is now called the poet laureate of the United States. There were the usual accolades: Bill Stafford was a poet whose plain language fitted his flatland Kansas sensibility. His poems were gifts to all Americans, not just to other poets or professors of literature.

There were other kind words: About the self-evident and the obligatory stories in his poems. About those poems' gifted reticence. Then something extraordinary was said. One of his children, his daughter Kit, I think, told us of her father's repeated advice to them as they were growing up: "Talk to strangers."

Not far from where I live when in Kansas, and about the same distance from where Bill Stafford grew up, there is a high school in a town of about a thousand that has a video security system of which they are especially proud. I had been asked to be part of a literary program there, and I noticed the surveillance camera in the room we used. Later I saw the black-and-white glow of monitors in the school's office. I watched pictures of the gymnasium (empty this autumn Saturday), various hallways (also empty), our meeting room (adults milling around drinking coffee), and finally an outside shot: the wide prairie as background, a small Kansas town in the foreground.

One of the school's officials and a parent stopped to say that you couldn't be too careful these days, what with Columbine and Amber Alert. Bad things happen in schools. And out of schools. Better to be vigilant than sorry. When they left, I could see them on the monitors as they walked across the lawn. They talked for a moment over the bed of a pickup truck and then drove off— safe, I suppose, in the knowledge that someone might have been watching them.

I was Bill Stafford's student because I learned from him about writing and life: Do it all and do it all now. The beginning may not be the beginning. The end may not be the end. These aphorisms applied not only to his craft and mine, but to the way we lived.

Over the years we wrote back and forth: letters, postcards, copies of our work. As he was one of the most prolific American poets of the 20th century, I got plenty more of the latter than he did. No matter how far apart we were, Bill in Oregon and me in Kansas or in Europe, he would sign off with "Adios" or "Cheers." Then, as if we were just across the pasture, he'd add: "Stop on by." My feeling now is that when I'd get to him, a little windblown and dusty from the walk over, he'd want to know if I'd met any strangers on the way, and what stories they had to tell.

What kind of America have we become when it seems stupid to give the same advice to our children that Bill Stafford gave his? Talk to strangers? Have we come to believe that surveillance cameras in the high schools of tiny towns are necessary to teach our students the eternal vigilance they'll need to live in towns beyond their own? Or in their own? What with Columbine and Amber Alert. Or would we be better off to listen to Bill Stafford from his poem "Holcomb, Kansas"?

> Now the wide country has gone sober again.
> The river talks all through the night, proving
> its gravel. The valley climbs back into its hammock
> below the mountains and becomes again only what

it is: night lights on farms make little blue domes
above them, bring pools for the stars; again
people can visit each other, talk easily,
deal with real killers only when they come.
Unless, of course, we have all become real killers.

There may be no reclaiming Bill Stafford's vision of America,
but don't you remember that once upon a time, in his plain voice,
he spoke for you?

The Last Tank of Gasoline in America

And it came to pass that the last tank of gasoline in America was to be found in Bly, Kansas.

"It's in Cal Hubbard's '89 GMC pickup," says the Big Government Farmer over coffee at the co-op.

We are all Government Farmers, but some of us more so than others.

"Too bad Cal passed away without getting to use it," says the farmer who pumped the last irrigation water.

That was a year ago. Television from the rest of America came to watch. They didn't know about our tank of gasoline.

"I heard he told Debbie Lee about it just before he died," says one of us.

Some of us have gone to Debbie Lee's to look at Cal's pickup parked in a barn where he used to keep horses. Those were the days. And they are again.

"Why do you suppose he didn't use it?" asks the Last Irrigator.

"Cal was always saving things," says Debbie Lee from the doorway.

With people walking everywhere these days, you don't hear them coming. If it would rain, you could hear the grass grow.

Debbie Lee is flowers on the windowsill to us. We all had crushes on her when we were young. Even now.

"Some coffee, Debbie?"

"Sure," she says.

Outside you can hear doves in the cottonwood trees. We've had enough morning dew that there might be a good pheasant hatch. And with no hunters coming from the cities to shoot them, we expect they'll flourish. Some of us will go back to hunting on horseback.

"What you going to do with it?" says one of us to Debbie. "The tank of gas."

"I'm thinking I'll drive to Kansas City and buy myself a pickup load of what I don't need," she says.

You have to know Debbie to know she's smiling to herself for putting us on.

"That would be the place to go," says the Government Farmer. "There's more of what you don't need in Kansas City than what you do."

"Or maybe I'll just drive around like there's no tomorrow," she says. "Looking at the cars stalled on the highway where they ran out of gas."

You still can't see her smiling.

"How about you siphon it into jars and sell them as souvenirs?" says one of us. "You could use labels like on wine bottles. Bly Gas, 2010. Special Reserve."

"What would Cal want us to do?" asks one of us after a moment.

Cal Hubbard was the best among us at guessing the future. Not if it was going to rain in a week or not, or if the price of cattle was going up or down. But at seeing ahead in life—as if life were more than what you bought with your money.

"He told me what to do with it," says Debbie. "It was the last thing he said."

We don't know this part of the story. She looks into her coffee. Then:

"He said, 'Do no more harm,'" says one of us. Debbie Lee looks up.

Now she's smiling where we can see it. We've made a good guess because it's what Cal would say when he'd head out for his day's work: "Do no more harm," raising his index finger at the word "more."

"But he didn't tell me how to go about it," says Debbie, looking at us as if we have the answer.

We are quiet again. Then:

"Do no more harm," one of us says after a moment, hitting the "more" the way Cal used to, index finger and all.

"Do no more harm," so say we all, Debbie Lee smiling to think of what good might come of Cal's last words now that they are what we say in the face of not knowing what to do with the last tank of gasoline in America—and so much else these days as well.

It's a start that at least it's quiet.

"Committee Meeting"

'It Was Snowing...'

Three of us are gathered here in Bly, Kan., at the co-op, to talk about the snow. It has been coming down in thumb-sized wet flakes, but by afternoon the sky will be white with tiny dots, giving the impression we have lost our horizons. The ground is still warm, so the snow will melt into the pastures. If it gets thick enough—and it will—it will fill the shallow wells we have for our livestock and homes. Maybe even the creeks will run when spring comes.

"A milllon-dollar snow," says one of the men. "If you count snow as cash on which we'll earn interest next spring."

"And a couple years beyond that," says the second man, "if we didn't have a debt to the drought."

It amuses us to think of snow as money.

We take our gloves off the propane stove, put on our coats and head for the door. We are off to move hay, check stock tanks, get wood in for the stoves, and before night park the pickups pointing toward where we might go the next day. We don't know it yet, but by morning we won't be going anyplace soon. Some of us in the country will be a week digging out.

"'It was snowing, and it was going to snow,'" I say as we step outside.

. . .

A man on a farm just outside of Bly is Steve Reuber. When the snow lets up, he gets into his 1962 John Deere 4010 with a front-end blade and heads toward Bly. The county can't get down here yet, but Steve can, so he does. We are a four-dirt-street tic-tac-toe of a town. That plus the Oil Road that leads to the U.S. highway. Steve has been plowing our streets—and our driveways—for 20 years. Same tractor. Same Steve.

"He's better than government," is what we say.

This year he'll take extra care to clear the streets all the way to the mailboxes, because otherwise our mailman, Gene Wurm, will have to get out of his car each time to make his delivery. Mr. Wurm is past 80 and we don't want him to take a fall. Most of us out here are old, and we are mindful of each other that way: Quick to hurt, slow to heal.

. . .

"It was snowing / And it was going to snow."

It's a line from the poet Wallace Stevens. When I am not who I am in Bly, I am a teacher who knows about poets. The men here understand that and don't hold it against me.

"It's not something we'd say," says the man who mentioned the milllon-dollar snow.

"I read 'Snow-Bound,'" says the other. "In school."

" 'The sun that brief December day / Rose cheerless over hills of gray, / And, darkly circled, gave at noon / A sadder light than waning moon.'"

"If you say so."

"And this is Robert Frost," I say:

"'Whose woods these are I think I know. / His house is in the village though; / He will not see me stopping here / To watch his woods fill up with snow.'"

By now we are at our trucks.

"Frost isn't talking to us either," says the man who was taught Whittier. "We don't have woods, and nothing 'fills up' except roads and draws with drifts."

Gene Wurm goes by on the Oil Road heading to Bly.

"It is money and it is going to be money," I say, looking around.

We are quiet for a moment. We all know the sound of snow in the wind, but you can't name it.

"Better your other poetry for who we are," says the first man.

I am thinking of drifts, of Steve Reuber, of the hand-pump wells we will be using the next few days because the power lines are down. No phones. No television. Wood smoke in the gray mornings. Snow as snow.

Wind, Water, Fact, and Fiction

When I was a young reader of novels in Kansas, I thought Don Quixote had a better view of the world than Sancho Panza: those were not windmills on Spain's distant hills but real knights in real armor ready to do real battle. Cervantes understood: no knights, no adventure; no adventure, no story. Windmills might be useful for pumping water out of the ground or grinding grist for polenta. But they were of better use for baking fiction. Not that I knew that then, but I knew something.

On the other hand, at about the same age I took Huck Finn's view of the world: Tom's robbers and funerals and jewels in Tom Sawyer and, at the end of Huckleberry Finn, his perpetual freeing of Nigger Jim from an imaginary prison using rules from only the finest romances was a silly fantasy conjured by the same Tom Sawyer who was trying to con me into whitewashing his fence: Not so fast.

To Huck the real world was real enough: the mark of Pap (a cross in the left boot-heel to keep off the devil); the sights and sounds and smells of the Mississippi that envelop the raft as it floats down river (*Toward night it began to darken up and look like rain; the heat lightning was squirting around, low down in the sky, and the leaves was beginning shiver . . .*); the ball of lead the woman in St. Petersburg tosses at Sarah Mary Willlams (a.k.a. Huck Finn) in his dress and that he catches like a boy, closing his legs instead of spreading them to open her skirt. And in that same scene the test Huck passes over how horses and cattle stand up (I, too, passed the test; but then I was from Kansas). Finally, there was the debate in Huck's mind about the fate of Jim that seemed especially real to me when I was young. With Mark Twain's help, both Huck and I passed that test as well. The lights of the Enlightenment glowing bright in a nineteenth-century American novel. Not that I knew that then.

Today I live part of my life in Western, Kansas (the W is always capitalized as if that section of the state not only has its special ecology and physiognomy—which it does—but also other singular traits, both political and cultural: the world is five thousand years old; a man's wife is called The Wife; the creeks are dry; the rest of America is called The Rest of America—all capitalized as if it were a country elsewhere—and the word Kansas means "People of the South Wind").

"It will blow the wheat out of the ground if this keeps up," says a farmer coming into the Bly Co-Op, where the Committee to Save the World meets sporadically over cowboy coffee and breakfast rolls baked by The Wife. We are trying to push winter into spring. The gardeners among us have set their tomatoes; the onions are starting up. Radishes too. Even though we know there might yet be a late blizzard in the works.

"I got fences so full of tumbleweed I can't see that I've got fences," says a buffalo rancher, beating the dust out of his hat and sitting down. The wind has been blowing hard for a week: night and day.

In the next hour or so we will solve the various problems of Bly and Whitewoman County, Kansas, plus a few for The Rest of America, if only they'd listen. And some shared difficulties as well: the high price of oil among them.

"We are," says the wheat farmer as the lights in the co-op blink off and on with a gust that rattles the windows, "the Saudi Arabia of wind."

I live another part of my life in southwestern France. It is "ac" country: Bergerac, Pessac, Cadillac, Gensac. Water, water everywhere—as well as wine and eau de vie—and plenty of everything to drink. Even some towns and villages are drinkable: Cognac, Armagnac. And with the water are mills: Moulin de Clotte, Moulin de Piqueroque, to name two near my small seventeenth-century stone house tucked into a hillside at the juncture of three Côte de Castillon vineyards.

This part of France is but a three-hour drive from the Spanish border, and from there another half-day's drive to the plain of La Mancha (the rain in Spain does not stay mainly on the plain). I have made that drive more than a few times over the previous twenty years; from San Sebastián (where Hemingway packs off Robert Cohn and Lady Brett Ashley, leaving Jake Barnes and the rest of the grand crew in Paris drinking up and down Boulevard Montparnasse), to Bilbao and its Gehry Guggenheim, then south toward the route the innkeeper proscribes for Don Quixote as he "sallies forth": Granada, Salamanca, Segovia, Seville (where on my most recent trip I got a haircut, of course. Fiction into fact).

What I have noticed driving though Spain are the growing number of windmills; at first, a few on distant hillsides that took me by surprise so that I was not quite sure (unlike Sancho) what they were. Then more. And a few years ago along the Costa de la Muerte, there was a long line of them like sentinels looking out over the Atlantic. For what? Wind.

This year when I made the drive, I saw battalions of windmills north of Burgos. Then small armies farther south toward Madrid. Added together they formed a crusade of windmills, assembled not to drive infidels out of the country but instead to keep Spaniards at home in clean and well-lighted places.

There were as well along the highways the celebrated huge cut-outs of black Spanish bulls, complete with very Spanish cojones. I am told that a few years ago someone in the government at Madrid decided it was a bit much, all these billboards of bulls with balls, and starting taking them down. But the Spaniards like their bulls and protested. Apparently they like their windmills as well, if I am to judge by the growing number of them. And my guess is that not even Don Quixote could mistake the modern windmill for a knight-errant. I take that back: He could and would. To me they look like ballet dancers: graceful in both design and movement. Utile beauty. It has a ring to it.

When you read literature in college, you read for theme or meaning, not for wind and water. You are taught that Sancho and Huck are realists; Tom and Don Quixote are romantics. That the theme of Huck Finn and Don Quixote is the "clash" (I recall this from one of my professors) of two "worldviews." Fact versus Fiction. Which world is yours? was the explicit question that came of our literary study, and no doubt the topic for an assignment: There is something about teaching books that can steal their souls. Nothing is the same after you explain it.

As to meaning, my view these days is that "meaning" in novels is a moral matter; that is, a question of human activity. Of ethics. The habit of behavior. Huck and Don Quixote and Tom and Sancho "come alive" insofar as we understand that the way they walked and rode and floated through their world has meaning in ours. That gets us past realists and romantics to a narrative trail where we come upon the mark of a boot, knights as windmills, the plain of La Mancha and its goatherds and songs of dead shepherds, and what a celebrated St. Louis poet called the strong brown god of a river. These and other facts of life: Horses stand front legs first. We, like good novels, are made of local detail. Fact into fiction. Fences of tumbleweed.

In western Kansas we are running out of both water and people. The creeks are dry. To irrigate the corn we pump water out of various underground rivers: aquifers they are called. Rain, as it turned out, did not follow the plow. Not the way the settlers followed the free land. Now the great grandchildren of those settlers are leaving. For the city. Where there is water. At least in plastic bottles. Western Kansas is not "ac" country. Our irrigation wells are run by oil.

In a number of the townships and counties across the western plains, there are fewer of us on the land than when the frontier closed. The Butane Stars of the farmyard lights have gone out. Bly has no stores. The bank closed a few years ago. The co-op is only open mornings, and not all mornings. The Committee to Save the World has fewer members every year, and not long before it has no place to meet. Even the grain train that runs by the south edge of town seems lonely. Nobody's here. Only the wind.

"The Chorus Line"

I Get A Horse

"The schoolteacher who writes about us says he's going to get a horse to ride to town," says Mencken.

"What for?" asks Ed Earl.

"Groceries. Brown's Hardware. Potted flowers like he puts out in spring."

"I mean why?"

"Save money on gas, I'd guess. Frugality in general."

I am the schoolteacher Mencken Cody and Ed Earl Willlams are talking about. I am not there. It is a meeting of the Committee to Save the World, at the co-op in Bly, Kansas. It only takes two to have a meeting.

It is coming wheat harvest. Most of us don't have time right now to save the world, so it won't be long before Mencken and Ed Earl pile into their pickups.

Gas is crawllng toward $4 a gallon. Diesel fuel is crawling uphill as well. The high-dollar wheat these men hope to sell could take a bad hit if you count the price of the fuel to bring it in.

But for the moment they are mediating over coffee about what they've heard I'm going to do.

"For an idea it sounds a quart low," says Ed Earl.

"It's a quart you don't have to add to your crankcase," says Mencken. "Besides, it's turning the clock back to better days."

"Clocks run straight on," says Ed Earl. "That's why you push up daisies sooner or later."

"I had a horse as a boy," says Mencken. "Rode it to school a couple of times for the pleasure of it. I had to leave early and come home late. The world goes slower on a horse."

"Three to four miles an hour," says Ed Earl. "Slow even for government work. Time's money."

"My dad used to say the outside of a horse is good for the inside of the man. It jiggles your innards for exercise. Besides, what's time to a horse?"

"Does he know about horses?" asks Ed Earl.

"I saw him riding the Holste horse the other day. He bounces off the saddle at a trot, but he doesn't steer a horse by pulling on one rein then the other like that woman from the East Coast did. He's got a proper saddle. Not a cut down model. He can ride. Worked cattle near Hays, I think."

They look into their coffee to study about me riding a horse to town and what kind of talk that will start.

"If he'd get a horse that could pull a wagon," says Ed Earl, "I'd ask him to pick up a few things and skip a trip to town. He could carry his potted flowers easier as well."

"It costs me $3 here and back to drive my truck," says Mencken.

"A horse costs something," says Ed Earl.

"Figure the farrier bill and the vet like tires and oil," says Mencken. "Figure feed like gas, though a round bale would feed a horse for a month. But let's say it's even. You save insurance."

"Only if you sell your truck," says Ed Earl. "Just sitting your pickup costs money every month like you were using it. A man would have to give up the use of his truck to come out ahead."

"A man loses the use of his pickup in this country and it's like losing the use of his ... ."

"Don't say it out loud," says Ed Earl. "He'll put it in what he writes and that will cause all kinds of trouble for us."

They are quiet for awhile. Others of the Committee to Save the World would have been here by now if they were coming. The coffee pot is foaming black goo at the bottom. There is sunshine in the work day ahead of us.

I am heading to the Oliva farm to see if they need me to drive their grain truck. As I go by the co-op I notice Ed Earl's and Mencken's pickups. But I have promises to keep.

"How's he going to write about what we said without him being here?" asks Mencken.

"Somebody will let him know," says Ed Earl.

"I hope by the time he tells on us he's got his horse," says Mencken.

"With a wagon," says Ed Earl, standing up to drive to town.

Committee To Save The World

The Committee to Save the World

"I walk what I know"
William Stafford

Toward the end of Gabriel Garcia Marquez's novel *One Hundred Years of Solitude*, Aurellano Buendia says to his brother Jose Arcadio: "Everything is known." Aurellano has been trying for some time to decipher the mysterious parchments (which turn out to be the novel itself) that were left many years before at the Buendia house by the gypsy Melquiades. A chapter or so later (just as the book comes to its end) Aurellano discovers the key to the parchments that allows him to learn not only the history of his family but his own fate—a fate that has him reading his own fate. However, a few pages before that happens, Aurellano repeats himself and again says: "Everything is known."

Each summer and into the early fall, my wife, the painter Kathryn Jankus Day, and I take up residence at L'Etang, a 16th-century farmhouse on the estate of Michael de Montaigne just outside the village of St. Michel de Montaigne. The farmhouse sits in a valley near a pond below the Montaigne castle—a huge Disney-like 19th-century Loire valley imitation built after a maid set fire to the original castle in order to steal some jewelry. Or so the local story goes. Montaigne would be skeptical.

Montaigne's tower (where he wrote his essays) did not burn, and to this day you can take a narrow, circular stone stairway up to his round study where there sits a full-sized cloth mannequin of Montaigne himself. He is arranged as if reading the facsimile of the Bordeaux edition of his essays on the table in front of him.

Above this faux Montaigne are carved into the ceiling beams his beloved quotations from the ancients: *I don't understand. I am in doubt.* (both from Sextus Empiricus) among more than 50 others: *The judgments of the Lord are a vast abyss (Psalm, 35); There is much to be said on all matters, both for and against.* (Homer, *The Iliad*).

It will bring you luck (again, according to local lore) if, during your visit to Montaigne's tower, you see on the stairs—or in the study itself—a black and white cat. The cat's name is Balzac. He was once our cat, a lost-and-found kitty we rescued from a poplar woods near St. Michel de Montaigne, a woods we have since named Bois de Balzac. My wife and I not only have our patois, we are the ones who started the story about spotting Balzac in Montaigne's tower bringing good luck. We believe in local lore.

Montaigne's famous inquiry is persistent: What do we know? As is its modern corollary: How do we know? The first question was Montaigne's motto: *Que sais-je?* The second concerns our age of "expanding information," superhighways of information that race in an infinite number of lanes around the earth on cosmic beltways, complete with cloverleafs and exits—Paris, Rome, Athens, Bombay, Hong Kong, Los Angeles, Chicago, New York, St. Michel de Montaigne, Bly, Kansas—all going faster by far than "break-neck speed," a phrase my mother would use to describe cars that passed our two-door Champion Studebaker as my father drove the R&P speed limit *(Reasonable and Proper)* on the roads of rural Kansas. Where are they going at "break-neck speed?" my mother would wonder. What madness is it? my father would reply.

Where are we all going at our 21st-century cosmic pace?—a pace that is not only to be contrasted with the R&P limits of 1950s Kansas roads, but with the walk-along rate of the Dordogne River that flows in the valley below Montaigne's tower: past the village of Lamothe, Montravel, then west to Castillon, Branne, Libourne and Fronsac—after which it joins the Gironde near Bourg. Then to sea. Where is the strong brown god of the river going? At what speed? Are we flowing with it? What do we know?

Does it mean something to how we know that it would have taken Montaigne four days on horseback to follow the Dordogne to Bourg and back in order to learn—and return with—the news that the grape harvest along the Côte de Bourg was just as bad as it had been for the Côte de Castillon? Does it make a difference to what we know that my father had to drive to see my uncle (who had no phone) to tell him of a death in the family? And to return with my uncle who wanted to stay with us that night because, as my mother said, he was feeling "mortal,"—and that that was the first time I had heard that word and was afraid to ask its meaning. Is there a ratio of speed to knowledge? Of information to knowledge? Of information to ignorance? Which of these ratios are literal? Which are inverse, ironic? What do we ever know? Seeing Balzac brings you good luck. If you say so.

I like Montaigne's way of thinking. In college I came to study him—as perhaps we all did—as the *père* of the essay. He was a master of "form." There were forms of literature in those days: novels, poems, short stories, essays. We were taught that the French word *essai* meant "to try," "to attempt." I don't remember any of us asking what we were to "attempt" when we took to writing our own essays; but over the years, it has occurred to me that in main we are to try to think. Not so much to "reason"—as if an essay were a pudgy syllogism—but to think in a contemplative way, a tentative way. An essay as a walk along a road taken in search of a discovered thought provoked by a singular image: the black bird in the cedar limbs just as it is beginning to snow—and is going to snow.

In this way we let our words discover our reason. Is it a way of knowing? Maybe. Is it a way of knowing everything? Maybe. It is a way of knowing yourself, then, to wit Montaigne: "There is nothing so contrary to my style as continuous narrative." Walks with stops as digressions. Not a four-day, but a six-day trip to Bourg and back if on the way you ride your horse up the steep hill to St. Emillon and consider what there is to see. The Dordogne in the valley below. Someone on horseback riding toward Bourg. An essay on the move. The essay as a form of life. A way of knowing as a way of life.

A number of years ago, a friend of mine told me he had read an article in which the author had observed that some societies unwittingly commit a kind of "suicide" (*autocide* or *autrocide* I think was the word the writer had coined) because affluence poisoned them in ways they did not understand: Lead pipes for Lexus-driving Romans. The best and brightest of the Dark Ages get themselves to monasteries. The author thought that America's autocide was "education." Or was it "television?" I can't remember. Or maybe my friend couldn't remember. Early senior moments. Would a revised version of the article (Montaigne revised his essays many times) now finger the Internet as an early symptom of autocide? Google searches? Power-point presentations? Palm pilots? Do we need a desk-top book to keep track? *American Autrocide: The Year in Review.* Maybe as an appointment calendar with enigmatic aphorisms: *September 13th. It seems as if something has been lost.*

Who was the author of the article on auto/autrocide? I don't know. Neither—after all these years—does my friend. A Google search does not find autrocide. For autocide there are 601 "hits," most of them having to do with killlng yourself by driving your car at break-neck speed onto the exit of oblivion. There are

641,000 references to lead pipes. Is 641,000 an inoculation against lead poisoning? Against television?

There is a theory these days that we will be better off as riders on the earth together if we understood that sometime in the recent past (with the invention of the Gatling gun, or antibiotics, or the Atom bomb, or the overhead projector, or cloning, or SUVs, or cyberspace) we crossed an invisible boundary into an alien Oz where we have more information than we need to live on the planet, which in turn means we don't know enough to know what is useful. Our lives now process and package the flotsam and jetsam of cyberspace, and like Charlie Chaplin in *Modern Times*, we can't keep up. We don't know when we got lost, much less where we are. We need to find the road back to black-and-white Kansas. We need a "limited world view." A lot of knowledge has become a dangerous thing: *Paradox. Irony. Mortal.* We learned these words (and their meanings) when our teachers had their degrees in English literature, not in Education "modules." It seems as if something has been lost.

The farm where we live below Montaigne's castle has no heat (save for two huge fireplaces that were there in Montaigne's time), so my wife and I usually leave the Dordogne by late October or early November—although one year we stayed until January, partly to see if we could do it, and partly because I had been asked to give a series of lectures in Bordeaux (a three-day trip by horse, an hour by my two horse Citroen Deux Chevaux) from L'Etang. We made it through the winter, although my colleagues at the university probably wondered at the less-than-faint smell of wood smoke in my clothes.

When we leave L'Etang in southwestern France, we migrate to a semi-ghost town in northwestern Kansas that I have in my writing named Bly, partly to protect its privacy and partly because I like fiction as well as fact—maybe more. The winters in Bly can be

fierce, but our modest Sears and Roebuck House is fully heated
by a wood stove we have come to call Henry. Like the characters in *One Hundred Years of Solitude* during the amnesia plague,
we tend to give the inanimate objects of our life proper names,
thus the vacuum cleaner we inherited from an aunt is Dead Aunt
Margaret, while an overstuffed reading chair is Gertrude Stein,
and our pickup truck is Bucephalus. Neither of us can remember
why our wood stove is Henry. Some things are not known.

I am tempted to write that Knowing and Ignorance (should
I write Enlightenment and Superstition?) in western Kansas are
different from Knowing and Ignorance in southwestern France.
But I know men and women on the High Plains who think there
were no Jews in the Twin Towers on September 11th, that Jesus
ascended to heaven (à la Remedios the Beauty in Marquez's novel),
and that the Environmental Protection Agency of the United
States government is a bureaucratic contrivance bent on telling
farmers and ranchers how to live their lives. Half a continent and
an ocean away, I know men and women who think the Dreyfus
affair was a plot by the Rothchilds, that there were no Muslims in
the Twin Towers on September 11th, and that because of the steep
French taxes, private property has vanished: You rent your cha-
teaux from the government in Paris. There is high-grade xeno-
phobia in this. Both the French and the Americans are famous for
it. Tend your own garden, and don't talk to strangers.

All of which prompts the question: What do we do about what
we don't know?—especially considering that we may not know
what we don't know. There are other questions: What is the rela-
tionship between "knowing" and enlightenment? Information
and knowing? Ignorance and superstition? Is superstition the
same as religion? Again: Does an increase in information paradox-
ically lead to an increase in ignorance? And if we want to know
less (and therefore be able to manage what we know), isn't it true
that enlightenment, not to mention science, brings us more and

more knowledge in the first case and more and more information in the second? Would it then follow that a "limited world view" is presently held by those who believe in the houris?

I am not a "thinker." Nor am I a "problem solver." I do not have a "world" view, limited or otherwise. I am by nature a story-teller. That is, stories happen to me. I write to retell them, just as Montaigne wrote to study himself. I walk what I know. Along my narrative way, some of my characters think. Sometimes they think about problems. Sometimes they solve problems. Or they stand by and watch others solve problems (as Chekhov has taught us, they also serve who stand and watch). My characters are, therefore they exist. They move through the world around them. It is my plea-sure to create that world and in so doing, create them: tall ranchers in battered pickup trucks; widows in dying Kansas towns, Prairie Populists living on hardscrabble ranches. There are days (and they increase in number as I get older) when I think my stories are the only reality I know, because in them, I know everything. I have cheated creation by creating something myself. I do not worry about knowing too little or too much. Like Mozart in *Amadeus*, I use just as many notes as necessary—neither too few nor too many. My world is circumscribed. I know what I know. Or to steal from Montaigne: "Others shape the man; I narrate him."

Having created worlds I might be—and my fellow storytellers (poets and filmmakers and playwrights) might be—just the people to ask when it comes to questions of how the world works. Or doesn't. We have solved the problems of our limited worlds, and in so doing, we have reason to conclude, we have learned a few useful things (Plato notwithstanding) about the reality outside the cave of our fiction—if in fact it exists.

Let no reader willfully misunderstand me: I am not saying that those looking for answers to the questions I have posed should ask me—or any other creator of fictive worlds. Not at all. You should ask our characters. They know more than we do. We are limited deities. In a collective way, they have the answers. Talk to them. Paradox, oxymoron.

It is from Oedipus through Job and on to Hamlet and Emma Woodhouse, then to Molly Bloom and Huck Finn and Bartleby and Aurellano Buendia (with Montaigne as editor) that I suggest the following three ways to address the problem of what to do about what we don't know.

First, à la the Prince of Denmark, we dither. Since we don't know for sure what we are doing, we might as well stand down stage for awhile talking to ourselves in hopes that the answer turns up somewhere later in the play. Modernity has after all made our lives better in a number of ways, from pasteurized milk to the civil-rights movement, to heart valves, and it has a decent record for "fixing" problems, at least the ones we can understand. That's why you talk to yourself. There is an old adage among doctors that if they listen to the patient long enough he will tell them what is wrong with him—not that the patient necessarily knows, but the doctor does. In the meantime, best to let some scenes pass while we wait for a sign on how to disturb the universe.

Second, we could prefer to do nothing. (Which may or may not be the same as doing no harm—my mantra). But what is doing nothing? Will something come of nothing? In practical terms, does "doing nothing" mean living (at least here in America) with great frugality? *Use It Up. Wear It Out. Make It Do. Do Without.* What would that accomplish? Would living in the Western World's most prosperous 21st-century capitalist society as if we were 19th-century French peasants—raising our own pig, making our own wine, force-feeding geese with corn for *foie gras* to barter at the Castillon Monday market—be a way to vaccinate ourselves against contemporary autrocide? Or would it only confirm yet another of Montaigne's maxims: *Do not consult your desires to know your needs.*

For the inoculation to take, would not everyone have to turn down the heat? Turn off the air conditioners (they steal summer, don't they?). Make teenagers bike to school. (God, Dad!). Walk to my uncle's house—and walk him back to ours. Stop driving to get a pack of cigarettes. Stop smoking. Cease vacations (the word "vacant" is in there somewhere). Stop shopping (a friend once defined "shopping" as walking through a mall looking for something you don't need and don't want—until you see it, at which point you buy it even though you still don't need it). Cease and desist getting and spending. Go through the world at R&P speed.

Isn't it the business of American culture (and now Global Capitalism) to confuse you about your desires and your needs, so that your desires are your needs? Isn't it the goal of the American Way of Life that in the end you are bereft of needs? And that in getting and spending we increase our powers? What madness is it to use it up, wear it out, make it do, do without? Isn't break-neck speed the road to productivity? How can we have freedom without shopping? Besides, if we turn off the engine of turbo capitalism, all the advertisements in *The New Yorker* (for David Yurman "Timepieces"—which I assume are "watches"; and Prada—a company I assume sells clothes; and Kenneth Cole—who, in the recent issue of the magazine, seems to be selling chain saws to left-handed women) would be transformed into popular history. *The New Yorker* would lose readers, but academia would gain a course: "Contemporary Insignificant American History: What Once Was and No Longer Is. A Three Credit Seminar. Power-point Presentations." Does this add up to a "limited world view" or just a "limited world"? It turns out that the Book of Job, through *One Hundred Years of Solitude* had more questions about answers than answers for the questions. Welcome to fiction.

The third option is Oedipus's solution: Do something. But what? Remember, we are addressing the following problem: We don't know enough to know what to do to survive because (*en masse*) we know too much to know what we need to know. So let's do something. I repeat myself: What? Perhaps doing nothing was really doing something in drag. Or dithering in drag. Even though what we did was stop doing, doing, doing. Is that the same as doing something? Or doing nothing? Are these the right questions? And even if they are, will we know the right answers when we see them? Are we in danger of not being able to see our way out of an Escher perspective to the Yellow Brick Road of our future? Do we already live in a monastery with lead pipes? Do we dare to eat a peach? We could pray. But for what? Enlightenment? And to whom? Gods don't like Enlightenment.

Montaigne writes: "We must remove the mask from things as from persons." He also notes: "Every man has in himself the whole form of human nature." What is the mask? Gide, in writing about Montaigne, asserts that "…as the mask belongs more to the country and the period than to the man himself, it is above all by the mask that people differ, so that in the being that is really unmasked, it is easy to recognize our own likeness."

I quote these passages because they seem wise. I am not sure wisdom can solve problems, nor am I sure wisdom can be a feature of a large democracy—much less a world with huge populations of illiterate, semi-literate, and, increasingly, rampant religious barbarians. In fact I am pretty sure it can not—mainly because wisdom comes from self-knowledge, and poverty, religion, and prosperity are barricades to self-knowledge. And as far as I can tell most of the world is thus divided: into three parts.

In Bly, Kansas, we are down to four dirt streets, bad water, 20 old cottonwoods, a "past tense dog" as mayor, an owl or two, deer on the edge of town, wild turkeys in the middle of town, twenty or so of us denizens scattered around in houses next to vacant lots next to empty houses—plus one business: The Farmers and

Ranchers Co-Op down by the grain train tracks on the south edge of town. It is at this Co-Op where The Committee To Save the World meets. Mornings, usually.

The Committee to Save the World has between 10 and six-billion members. That is, anyone is automatically a member who stops by for coffee, takes a seat in one of the broken-down chairs that line the east wall of the Co-Op's office, and is willing to tell and listen to stories. If not stories, then a good ranch joke will do.

Even though the entire world is invited, the Committee's deliberations have so far attracted only about a dozen members (depending upon calving season, blizzards, wheat harvest, and prairie fires). Some days none of us are there, but that does not mean we have not met. Where none or some of us are gathered, we are The Committee To Save the World. In addition to this motto (not inscribed on the peeling plaster ceiling of the office), we have three rules: First, there shall be no agenda. Second, no one shall be in charge. Third, nothing shall be decided. A couple of years ago I tried to add Everything is Known as a kind of coda, but, as one wheat farmer pointed out, that would require deciding something and thus be in violation of rule three. There followed the joke about the Western Kansas rancher who had gone to hell where he met his banker, now the right-hand man to the devil.

Over coffee and sometimes a breakfast cake "the wife" has sent along, The Committee To Save the World tackles only small insolvable problems (what to do about the local hippie's dogs that are running through Bly these days and killing cats and chickens—as opposed to what to do about the local hippie, much less "hippies worldwide"). Our solutions are stories about what others have done about free-running dogs (or once, a free-running pig). Some dogs have been shot; some have been caught and taken to the local pound; others have been loaded into pickups and driven out to the great sweep of pastures north and west of Bly to fend for themselves. The pig was roped and roasted as part of "Bly

Days," a summer festival that on that year featured a T-shirt with "Hogs in Heat" printed underneath a silk screen of Satan roasting the pig. Or so the story is told.

The pigs and chickens and cats and dogs and hippies of Bly are not connected to the larger world. The rain is local, ergo so is the world. I once asked a widow who had lived in three sod houses before she got a frame one if she recalled October 29th, 1929; it was when the stock market crashed in New York City. "We had our own troubles that day," she said, and went on to tell a story about it.

A few years ago I asked the members of the Committee to Save the World if there had ever been a Mercedes in Bly. We have our "strangers" in town—but not many. Sometimes people from Denver or Kansas City take the river road east out of Blaze (also a real town with a faux name) as a "scenic detour," and so pass through Bly on their way to the main east-west road, and then to home. But that's about it. Few strangers, many wild turkeys.

"Yes," said one rancher. There had been some silence after I posed my question. Everybody was trying to remember. "Yes," the rancher said again. "There was a Mercedes in Bly. 1972. But he was lost."

1972. Is that the year when we all lost our way? *A Clockwork Orange* and *The French Connection*? The mining of Haiphong harbor. George Wallace is shot. Angela Davis. *Ms. Magazine*. The first baseball strike. The Gray Panthers. The Russian wheat sale scandal. Bobby Fischer. "Peace is at hand." "A third-rate burglary." *The Last Picture Show*. The list seems no more dire than any other year. Modernity or not.

Montaigne writes: I would not believe it had I seen it myself. Here he is more than skeptical. More than wondering if he is playing with his cat or his cat is playing with him. It is not bemusement that colors these words. Nor even balance. It is the awareness that the mind that searches (tries, attempts) must set aside certainty.

He knows that we seek not the answers, but ourselves. All solutions are limited. We are not. Everything is known.

Epilogue

I wrote most of these pieces for the popular press. The exceptions are "The Committee To Save the World" and "I Look Out for Ed Wolfe and "Parts of Their Night," the two eulogies for my teachers. Reading them over I was struck by how much the craft of fiction (I also write novels, and long and short stories) shapes this work. Like most writers I tell "stories." But when my mother used that word (as in "Don't tell me any stories, now"), she meant fibs or lies—white or otherwise. I am in accord with Katharine Ann Porter ("The Route of *The Last Cattle Drive*,") who noted that she will try to tell the truth but it will come out fiction. Fair warning: I am not reporting stories. I am telling them.

That said, I like the kind of truth I am telling: Kansas, where many of these pieces take place, exists outside the world of Judy Garland and William Allen White. The Committee to Save the World did meet once upon a time in Bly, Kansas, which does not exist—sort of. As a boy, I once hit stones as baseballs into a vacant lot outside of Merriam, Kansas, and into the Mediterranean along the Almalfi Drive ("Radio Games"). However, William Stafford did not tell me to talk to strangers ("Talk to Strangers and Stop on By"); I heard his daughter say it was advice he had given his children. It sounds like Bill. It sounds like something he might have said to me. Maybe he did.

My teachers—Edgar Wolfe and Edward Ruhe—were both as helpful to me when I was a young writer as I claim they were. Stanley Elkin and I did have that conversation about his health in San Francisco ("Look Out for Ed Wolfe"). Ed Ruhe was as furious about Richard Nixon as he was flummoxed about what kind of car he drove ("Parts of Their Night").

Then what's not true?

One answer is: That's for me not to know and you not to find out. Another answer is: Everything is true because I made it up. And a third answer is: I've told parts of these stories in one way or another (rearranging bits of time and place) for so long I couldn't tell you if you paid me.

I take that back: if an editor wants to pay me for an essay on what is fiction and what is nonfiction in my writing, I'd be pleased to do the piece as long as it is understood it might come out fiction. More or less.

It is my pleasure to thank people for the help they have been in both the original writing and publishing of this work, and in the publishing of this collection. The list is not long, but it is true: Diane Landskroener, Leo and Bonita Oliva, Bob Thompson, Wes Jackson, Harris Rayl, Scott Bonz, Robert Stewart, Claire Whitehill, Fred Whithead and the late Richard Harwood.

About the Author

Robert Day's novel *The Last Cattle Drive* was a Book-of-the-Month Club selection. His short fiction has won a number of prizes and citations, including two Seaton Prizes, a Pen Faulkner/NEA prize, and Best American Short story and Pushcart citations. His fiction has been published by *Tri-Quarterly, Black Warrior Review, Kansas Quarterly, North Dakota Quarterly* and *New Letters* among other belles-lettres magazines. He is the author of two novellas, *In My Stead,* and *The Four Wheel Drive Quartet,* as well as *Speaking French in Kansas,* a collection of short stories.

His nonfiction has been published in the *Washington Post Sunday Magazine, Smithsonian Magazine, Forbes FYI, Modern Maturity,* and *World Literature Today.* As a member of the Prairie Writers Circle, his essays have been reprinted in numerous newspapers and journals nationwide, and on such internet sites as Counterpunch.

Among his awards and fellowships are an National Endowment to the Arts Creative Writing Fellowship, both Yaddo and McDowell Fellowships, a Maryland Arts Council Award, and the Edgar Wolfe Award for distinguished fiction. His teaching positions include The Iowa Writers Workshop; The University of Kansas; and the Graduate Faculty at Montaigne College, The University of Bordeaux.

He is past President of the Associated Writing Programs; the founder and former director of the Rose O'Neill Literary House; and founder and publisher of the Literary House Press at Washington College, Chestertown, Maryland where he is an Adjunct Professor of English Literature.